100 WAYS TO MANAGE BETTER

By

Carl Cogdill

ISBN-13: 9780615818474 (Custom Universal)
ISBN-10: 0615818471

Editor: Sarajoy Bonebright
    I cannot possibly thank everyone that made this book possible. Every manager that I have ever worked with or for has helped to develop me into the manager I am today. To all of you that I have had the pleasure of working with over the years, thank you.
    I do, however, wish to dedicate this book to the two people that have supported me the most throughout my career. I could never have completed this book without the support of my wife, Nicole, and my son, Chance.

TABLE OF CONTENTS

How to Manage Presentations Better   77

How to Manage Communications Better

How to Manage Yourself Better

FORWARD

I am not an expert on leadership or management. That is probably not the reassurance you want after purchasing this book, but the truth is that I do not view myself as an expert. I am very leery of people that proclaim to be experts, especially those that want to charge to share their expertise with me.

I have a Master's degree in Business Administration and was previously a commissioned officer in the United States Army. I completed most of the coursework for a Doctorate in Management at the University of Maryland before I took a job in Florida and gave up on that pursuit, with no regrets. I have worked in various leadership positions over the last twenty-plus years, and I could write a very lengthy list of professional accomplishments. I don't throw any of that out there to impress you—it does not impress me—but rather to assure you with all sincerity that I do not consider myself an expert, on anything.

Many experts use anecdotal evidence to support their conclusions. They will tell you something that they did and how wonderfully it worked. If it worked for them, then surely it will work for you. There are too many variables in most solutions for that logic to hold true. While there are a lot of commonalities in different leadership positions, there are also a lot of differences. The history of the company, the people you are working with, and your abilities are going to be very different from any other leader. Not to mention attitude. If your attitude stinks, I could give you all the advice in the world, and it may not help you at all.

What I am trying to do is offer you a variety of tools that I have used in managing over the years. Some of them may work for you, but many may not. You are not me. I am not you. There is no law saying that we have to lead exactly the same way. There is not just one right way to lead.

Why should you read this book?

Do you have a mentor who helps you unlock all the secrets of managing? If you do, I suspect you are in the minority. This book will serve as an added resource—a way to cross-check whether the advice you're getting squares with some of the latest views on enlightened management.

If you lack a mentor, consider this book a friendly substitute. While I cannot sit beside you and whisper tips in your ear for every situation you might encounter, I can give you plenty of practical advice on handling a range of situations that you'll no doubt face as a manager.

I don't want to mislead you; effective management requires more than reading this book and nodding with approval when you come across a tip or technique that appeals to you. You must apply what you read. I will provide you a variety of tools, but it will be up to you to decide *when* to use those tools. By sampling the tools you're about to learn, you can evaluate to what extent they may work for you, and you can then modify them as needed. People are not mathematical equations, so managing requires a very dynamic solution. As long as you commit to putting into practice what we're about to discuss, I promise your time spent reading this book will pay off.

Enjoy the book, and please don't hesitate to send me your feedback at carl.cogdill@gmail.com.

HOW TO MANAGE YOUR TIME BETTER

I think most people struggle with managing their time. I know that there have been points in my career where I felt completely overwhelmed. I felt I had too much to do and not nearly enough time to get it done. I blamed my lack of time for my poor financial situation, my unachieved goals, my lack of fitness, and any other problems I had in my life.

Have you ever been in this situation? Time is certainly a precious resource, but some people seem to get more out of a twenty-four hour day than others. I don't claim to be a time management guru, but I have tried a variety of different things in an attempt to be just a little more effective.

In this section, you will find the tools that I have used to help me improve my level of productivity, get the important things done, and still have enough time to have some kind of personal life. I am going to list several tips for you. Some of them may work for you, and others may not. I encourage you to experiment with each of them and see if they can help you to manage your time just a little better.

#1: Don't let your to-do list hamper your productivity.

I know a lot of people that keep a to-do list. In fact, I would venture to bet that most of the people I know keep a to-do list. How about you? Is there a to-do list on your desk? Keeping a to-do list is certainly a good practice, but it will not help you to maximize your productivity.

However, in fact, it may be hampering your productivity. How is this possible, you ask? If you write down a dozen or so tasks that you want to complete each day and then just start going about knocking them off one at a time, it is highly unlikely that you are operating at maximum efficiency. Documenting the things you need to do each day is a great first step, but in order to maximize your efficiency, you then have to prioritize those tasks.

While almost everyone I know keeps a to-do list, I am not sure I know many people that prioritize it each day. This means they look at their list each morning, and they will likely attack the easiest or most pleasant tasks first.

We tend to start with things we like to do or things we know we can knock out in fairly short order. Then, we can cross those things off and feel like we are accomplishing something. The problem with this logic is that those fast and easy tasks are rarely the ones that will give us the biggest productivity bang. So we spend the majority of our day working on tasks that will likely add little value to our personal or professional lives, and the next thing you know...? We have run out of time before we get to the big stuff! This is how we can convince ourselves that we do not have time to exercise or work on other tasks that we may have deemed "unpleasant."

Try to take your to-do list and prioritize the tasks on it. Do not consider the complexity of each task; just consider what would have the biggest impact on your productivity. If you have two tasks that would have equal impact then prioritize the one that you find least appealing. I find that by prioritizing things I don't like doing, I tend to be more productive. You will always find time to do the things that you like, but you have to make time for things you find unpleasant.

Brian Tracy wrote a book called *Eat That Frog*. The book explores the importance of prioritization. If you are not familiar with it, I would suggest checking it out. It can easily be read in an afternoon and certainly illustrates the importance of prioritization better than I have laid out for you here.

Don't just read this and shake your head in agreement. This is a call to action. Jot down everything that you need to get done today, and then write a number next to each thing on the list. Number one should be the most important thing that you can do today that will make the biggest difference in your life, personal or professional—something that will cause you to feel a great relief once it's done. Then, continue to prioritize the remainder of your list.

The next step is easy, get started on number one. Complete the list in order. If you do not get everything done today, carry over any remaining tasks to tomorrow, but prioritize tomorrow's list first thing in the morning. It may be that you do not get to some of your trivial tasks for several days. That's the point.

Try it. I think you will be pleasantly surprised at how well this works.

#2: Follow these five tips to make meetings more meaningful.

I am not a big fan of meetings—never have been and likely never will be. Over my twenty years of being a manager, I have declined far more meetings than I have attended. People in your organization that do not have a good grasp on their jobs or what the company does altogether, tend to schedule a lot of meetings. This is why I dislike meetings.

Some meetings are necessary, but they do not have to be a pointless waste of time that accomplishes nothing. If you have determined it would be absolutely beneficial to get a group of people together to discuss an issue, there are a few rules you can follow to ensure the meeting is productive and to increase the chances that people will attend your meetings in the future.

1. Limit the participants.

The more people present, the less likely the meeting will be productive. Who needs to be there? Who are the decision makers, and who are the people that are going to get things done? Those are the people you want at the meeting. Extraneous people are just going to slow the meeting down as they will not fully understand the concepts that are being discussed.

2. Have an agenda.

If you determine this meeting is necessary, make sure everyone understands the purpose. Make a list of everything that needs to be covered. If you expect some of the participants to present information, make sure they know what they are responsible for. If at all possible, distribute the agenda 24 hours before the meeting. The goal here is for everyone to completely understand what you are trying to accomplish so that they can come to the meeting prepared. If the participants have put thought into the meeting objectives prior to the meeting, it will tend to progress much more quickly.

3. Be punctual.

If the meeting is supposed to start at 10:00, start the meeting at 10:00. I have worked in several companies where meetings rarely started on time. As a result, managers were conditioned to show up to meetings late. The same is true for ending on time. If you want to increase the likelihood that participants will show up at your next meeting, make sure that you end on time.

Do not however, schedule "extra time" to ensure you accomplish everything. Stay on point to ensure that you accomplish everything. Scheduling extra-long meetings significantly reduces the chances that all of the necessary decision makers will show up.

Do not wait for participants that are not present at the start time. When it is time to start, you need to start. It is disrespectful to people that are prompt to wait for the person that does not show up on time. Assume that the late person is not coming and move on with the meeting.

4. Cover the most important things first.

Your agenda should be set up so that you are starting on the most important issue or problem. If you start to run out of time, you have at least covered the big items.

5. Document your conclusions and assign action items.

Keep notes from the meeting. You don't have to write down every word, but at least capture any conclusions and also any action items that are assigned to someone. If someone agrees to do something after the meeting, make sure you note what they are going to do, who is going to do it, and when they will have it completed.

After your meeting, shoot out a quick email that summarizes the major points and outlines the action items.

#3: Take a moment after your next meeting.

I read an article by psychologist Art Markman. His book, *Smart Thinking: Three Essential Keys to Solve Problems, Innovate, and Get Things Done*, uses his years of cognitive research to explain many of the self-limiting behaviors that we all exhibit on a daily basis.

What caught my attention in the article was a point Markman made about what we do during and after meetings. He warns against multitasking during meetings, such as checking emails. He goes on to explain that when you multitask during a meeting you're not really giving the meeting or your email the appropriate attention, and you are likely to get burned at some point. No argument here, but that was not exactly a revelation, as I have heard this many times.

What was far more interesting to me was one of the other points he made, about what we do after meetings. Markman believes that most of us tend to dive right back in to our email immediately following a meeting. Again, no argument here, as that is 100% correct in my case.

Markman suggests that this is a behavior that we should be looking to correct. He suggests instead that you should take a moment and capture what you believe were the three most important points from the meeting. When you jump right back into your email, you greatly reduce your chances of remembering anything relevant from the meeting.

#4: Exercise a little self-control.

I try to practice what I preach. I will tell anyone that is willing to listen that you need to write down your goals and then break them down into daily actions in order to accomplish them. It is a pretty simple recipe and one that I actually follow. I do not, however, have a 100% success rate on accomplishing my goals. Honestly, I have no idea what the percentage would be, but I think it is pretty good.

So what keeps me from having a 100% success rate? I would love to list out the dozens of reasons beyond my control of why I do not accomplish some of my goals, but I think it comes down to self-control.

Self-control comes down to the following three factors:

1. *You must have some sort of standards.*
   (You know what you should do.)

2. *You are aware of whether or not your behavior is meeting your standards.*
   (Are you doing what you should be doing?)

3. *You are able to correct inappropriate behaviors.*
   (You can stop doing the things you should not be doing.)

Writing down your goals and then breaking them down into daily actions will help satisfy point #1. If my goal is to write a book, then one of my daily actions may be to write 1,000 words per day. If I have put that task on my to-do list for today, I have accomplished factor #1. So far, so good.

As my day progresses, I will undoubtedly become aware of the fact that I am not doing any writing. I am instead surfing the net, playing Angry Birds, or engaged in some other activity that will help to advance mankind. Should I panic at this point? Of course not. There is plenty of time left in the day; I will get to it.

I have accomplished point #2. I am aware that my behavior is not meeting my standards. This is a good thing. Self-control takes three factors, and I have already accomplished two of them.

Eventually, I will get to a point in the day where there is no more room for procrastination. It is time to put up or shut up. Have you ever gotten to that point?

It is 9:00 p.m., and I need to start writing. This is about the time that I will start rationalizing with myself. Thoughts like, *You can write 2,000 words tomorrow!* start to creep into my head. Now I am faced with a decision: I can either get down to writing, or I can rationalize why I should just go to bed and start fresh in the morning. If I choose to go to bed, I have failed on point #3. I was not able to correct the inappropriate behavior.

So how do we increase our chances on factor #3? I like to publicize a lot of my goals. Knowing that other people are aware I am making bad choices is a big motivator for me. People can then ask me how I am progressing on my goals, and the added pressure helps me develop a little more personal accountability.

#5: Take a lunch.

I read an article on MSN about how America's lunch hour is endangered. Apparently, I am in the minority because I eat lunch every day. Not only do I eat lunch every day, but I usually eat at the exact same time every day: between 11:30 and 12:30. It is not that my job is not hectic and there are not a hundred demands for my time, but rather, I eat lunch every day because I think it is important.

Lunch is important for the following several reasons:

1. *You need a break.*

I find that my cognitive skills improve greatly if I take short breaks. I have worked through my lunch at some points in my career, and I have found that I am not as sharp in the afternoon if I work straight through the day. Take a few minutes to step away and eat, and then come back with new focus.

2. You need fuel.

A study published in the *Journal of Nutrition* found that doctors that skipped lunch tended to be more irritable and more tired, and they made poorer decisions than their well-fed peers.

The physicians themselves reported that inadequate workplace nutrition has had a significant impact on their personal wellness and their professional performance. I am no doctor, but it sounds like they concluded people need to eat lunch.

3. Skipping meals helps you to gain weight.

Your metabolic rates speed up by about 20-30% for a couple of hours after you eat. Small and frequent meals (that are low in calories) are the key to losing weight. I need all the metabolic help I can get, so I am eating lunch.

I work in a large corporation, so there are certainly many in my company that I believe would look down upon the practice of eating lunch every day. They wrongly assume that because they sit in meetings all day and get behind in their real work, everyone else should do the same.

In order to avoid having to explain the merits of lunch and good time management to each of these people, I instead find it easier to just schedule a meeting every day from 11:30-12:30.

Most days that my direct reports will file into my office, we will have a "lunch meeting." We may talk work, or we may talk current events, politics, or whatever else is on our minds. Sometimes we eat fast and get right back to work, and other times, the lunch has turned into a brainstorming session, where we have really come up with some great ideas.

One thing is for sure, I always return from lunch recharged and ready to go!

I like lunch. I like the social aspects of it, and I like the way it breaks up my day. If lunch is truly on the endangered list, I promise you, I will be one of the last holdouts.

What about you? Are you taking a lunch today?

#6: Get to work early.

There are some people that like to come into work early, and there are some that prefer to stay late if they need a few extra minutes to get things done.

I prefer to come in early. It means that I have to get up a little earlier, but on most days, it is worth it. I realize that not everyone can just get up earlier and come into work whenever they want to. You may have family obligations that prevent you from making it into the office early. If that is the case, I certainly understand, and please continue to do whatever works for you. If, however, you are a person that does have the opportunity to make it into the office a little earlier, I highly suggest that you give it a try.

There are a number of benefits, such as the following:

1. You can beat traffic.

If you work a normal day job, your commute can be a big part of your day. My commute takes about an hour, and the exact time that I leave my house can play a very large role in whether the commute will be ridiculously long or perhaps as short as forty-five minutes.

2. You can get in before your coworkers.

Probably, the thing I like most about arriving early is that there are very few people in the office that could potentially distract me. That first hour or two of the day is when I like to tackle the hardest tasks. They go much easier if I am not interrupted every ten minutes. Early morning generally means no interruptions.

3. You can plan your day.

I notice that when people come in a few minutes late, it tends to throw them off for the entire day. They never seem to recover and feel in control of their day.

The first thing I do each day is check my schedule, make my to-do list, and set my priorities. If I need to prepare anything for any of my meetings, I make sure that I have everything I need.

It is amazing how relaxed you feel when you have a plan of attack. It is definitely worth losing a few minutes of sleep to feel relaxed all day.

I think the majority of people I work with tend to work late as opposed to coming in early. Many stay later than I do, but very few come in earlier than I do. I don't know if I believe the early birds have an advantage over the night owls. I suspect it is more a matter of personal preference.

One thing I do not do when I get up early and come in to work is check my email. I usually try to focus on more cerebral activities and then switch to email later in the morning.

Are you an early bird or a night owl? When do you do your best work?

#7: Delegate the important tasks too.

Delegation is skill that needs to be mastered if you want to be an effective manager. I don't think delegation comes naturally to any of us. It is a behavior that takes time and effort to perfect. Giving your employees simple, tedious, and laborious tasks to complete does not make you a great delegator. When you are able to give up the complex tasks you are good at, that is when you have started down the path of being a great delegator.

A complex task that I am extremely good at is budgeting. I have very complex labor models I have built over the years that allow me to budget very effectively and easily. I can estimate the labor and operating expenses for my department with a high degree of certainty. I believe my ability to accurately and quickly budget is one of my greatest strengths.

Over the almost eight years that I have been in my current role, I have had to create a budget every year. That is eight different occasions that I could have spread some of my modeling and budgeting knowledge with my direct reports—eight different opportunities that I have failed to capitalize on. None of my direct reports would be capable of creating a departmental budget if I were to suddenly be removed from the picture. This is a huge failure on my part.

What really troubled me was that I could not easily figure out why I have failed to develop this talent in any of my team members. After some careful consideration, I have determined the reasons for this failure to be the following:

1. Complexity

The budget process itself is complex, and the labor models that I have built to support my budgeting process are even more complex. It would take a great deal of time to really educate someone on the process.

2. Speed

My windows for completing my budgets are usually very tight. It is a very intense process for a very short period of time. It is a high stress time already, so it would just add to the stress if I had to slow down and explain each step to someone else.

3. Responsibility

Ultimately the budget for my department is my responsibility. I am the captain of this ship, so it is really not a task that I should be delegating.

4. Interest

None of my direct reports has even remotely hinted to having any interest in the budget process, and I really don't think that it is something that you could easily grasp if you have no interest in it.

Those seem like pretty good reasons not to delegate something; however, after more careful consideration, I have decided that all four of those reasons are complete rubbish.

Here are the counter-arguments as to why.

1. Complexity

If you have a large and complex goal to complete, then you have to break it down into manageable tasks. This week, I am going to break the budgeting process down into much smaller learning modules, which my team and I can begin to go through in the very near future. I will feed it to them task by task. It may take us a while to achieve the goal, but this is a much better alternative than trying to teach them during the budget process.

2. Speed

The budget process may be fast and furious. All the more reason to teach them how to budget well before the process starts. I have been here for eight years; I think that would have been ample time to get them sufficiently trained.

3. Responsibility

I am ultimately responsible for the budget for my department. However, that does not mean that I personally have to complete every aspect of the budget process. I will spend the next six months getting my team trained on the budget process. In the fall, when we go to budget for the next year, I will have them complete the budget process as if I were not here. I will also independently complete the process. We can then compare notes, and it will serve as a much needed double check to ensure that everyone is using the correct logic.

4. Interest

If I understand the role of a leader, which is debatable, then it is up to me to generate that interest. Financial modeling and budgeting is not a skill set that a large percentage of the population has. I have the chance to give my team a gift that will help them to experience more job security and more job satisfaction, and it will greatly increase their chances of advancing in this or any other organization. If someone explained it to me like that, I would certainly be interested in learning more.

Here is what I think I have learned: I tend not to delegate tasks that will require a great deal of effort on my part to train someone else. The reasons why are irrelevant. The bottom line is that I am depriving my team of a chance to make a greater contribution to the company. In these tough economic times, I think I have a moral obligation to do whatever I can to increase their value to the organization.

My questions to you are as follows:

1. Is there anything you would like to learn more about that your boss could help with?

If one of my direct reports had approached me years ago asking to learn more about the budget process, I am confident that I would have spent the time to teach them more. Sometimes your boss needs a gentle nudge. Mention specific functions that you would not mind if they delegated to you.

2. *Is there anything you have failed to delegate to your team because the task is so complicated it would take too much time to train them, or is it a task you simply like to do?*

If so, I would ask you to reconsider. Learning new skills is a pretty big perk to any job. It also clearly demonstrates a dedication to your employees. I know I would appreciate a boss that took the time to mentor me. Be that boss.

#8: Schedule your day the right way.

There are certain points in the day that tend to be far more productive for me. I would not classify myself as a morning person, as I prefer to not have contact with humans for the first two or three hours of the day, but I would say I am more productive in the morning. I tend to do a lot of my writing in the wee hours of the morning; it feels like the words flow much easier at that point in the day.

In the afternoon, I tend to be more sociable but not as productive. I, therefore, try to arrange my schedule so I am working on the more cognitive tasks early in the day and the social tasks, such as meetings, after lunch. I am fortunate that I have a fair amount of control over my schedule, so I am able to execute this plan most days.

What about you? Have you ever really thought about when you are the most productive? I know many people that are a ball of energy in the evening hours, so that tends to be their most productive time. Your diet, stress levels, and sleep habits can all play into when you have the most energy, but I find that the times are fairly consistent for most people day in and day out.

Have you ever thought about when you are the most productive, the most energetic, the most cognitive, or the most social? Take a few minutes and think about it.

Once you have determined your answers, think about whether your schedule takes advantage of your natural energy cycles. If you tend to have the most energy in the morning, is that is when you are exercising? Should you try to schedule your meetings later in the day? For those that aspire to be writers, are there times in the day that it is easier for you to write? Are you taking advantage of those times?

I prefer to exercise in the mornings. I tend to be much more consistent when I do. If you find that mornings are not helping you stick to a workout routine, then try switching up to work out in the evening. Do the same with your writing routine. Try switching up the time of day you are attempting to write, if you are struggling.

Are you a night owl or an early bird?

#9: Schedule 45-minute meetings.

How did we get stuck on the concept of hour long meetings? It is likely due a programmer at Microsoft that made an hour the default setting on Outlook. Should our meetings last an hour? I would argue they probably should not as you need to have some time between meetings to physically get to the next meeting or to mentally change your focus.

Why not manually change your meetings to 45-minute meetings? I seriously doubt you cannot accomplish what you need in 45 minutes. Our meetings last an hour because we know that is how long we have.

You should have an agenda for your meetings. You should limit the participants. You should keep people on topic. You should document all action items and send out a recap. These are all good practices, but they can be challenging for folks to get into the habit of doing. Changing your hour long meetings to 45 minutes is not challenging at all. It is a very easy habit to pick up, and it gives you back 25% of your time.

Think about the repercussions. It will give you time to transition between meetings and all of your meetings should be able to start on time. This is a time management revolution that I want to be a part of. I am going to change all of my hour long meetings to 45-minute meetings.

#10: Think like a shark.

Sharks have to keep moving forward in order to survive. You do too, but you may not realize it. You likely have goals for your life. You want to drop a few pounds, save a few bucks, network more effectively, and finally get around to writing that book. So does everyone else, but 95% are never going to accomplish those goals. What makes you so special that you think you are going to succeed at accomplishing any of your goals?

You can greatly increase your chances if you think like a shark. Just keep moving forward. If you want to lose fifty pounds, your goal should not be to lose it all today. You goal for today is to just move forward.

If you have not been exercising, maybe you start an exercise program. Maybe you start drinking water instead of soda. Maybe you start including vegetables with every meal. The step forward you take is not as important as ensuring you are doing something to move forward with your plan.

Ask yourself the following questions:

- What can you do today to be a better manager?
- What can you do today to be a better writer?
- What can you do today to be a better parent?
- What can you do today to be a better friend?
- What can you do today to be a better person?

I am not telling you anything you do not already know, but sometimes we all need a reminder. In all honesty, it may be me that needed the reminder more than anyone.

Today is a gift; don't waste it. Turn off the television. Think like a shark, and keep moving forward.

#11: Take time for self reflection.

There are things I am good at, things I am not so good at, and a few things I really need to do a little more frequently. I imagine this is true for just about anyone. One of the things I need to schedule a little more time for is reflective thinking. It is almost a bit of a self-assessment, where you evaluate how things are going in your life. I talk to many people that are unhappy with certain, or perhaps all, aspects of their lives.

In almost every case, where I encounter someone that is in a "bad place," they almost always blame something external. Their boss is lousy, their spouse is crazy, or their kids just won't listen. Rarely do I hear any of these folks assess what their role in their current situation has been. For the most part, we are all victims of the decisions we make. Sometimes we make great decisions and good things happen, and sometimes we make poor decisions and are suddenly very unlucky.

Whatever the quality of your decisions has been lately, I would strongly encourage you to take a few minutes of time alone and assess where you are in life. Look at where you are professionally, personally, financially, spiritually, and any other way that you can think. Are you happy with where you are? If you are, take a moment and reflect on some of the decisions you made that got you to this happy place. This reflective thinking will help you have more confidence in your decision making skills.

What if you are not happy with where you are in some aspects of your life? I still want you to think about the decisions you made that got you to this point. It is difficult to learn from your mistakes if you do not own up to them, or take a moment to reflect on where you might have gone wrong and why.

Once you have taken a few minutes to ponder that, I want you to think about where you want to be and how to get there. If you want to be promoted, then what can you do to increase your chances? If you want to save more money, where can you cut back and save a few more bucks? If you want to have a better relationship with your spouse, what are you willing to do to make that happen?

If you are not spending any time reflecting back on the decisions you made, then I promise you that you are not reaching your full potential. You control your destiny. You control the decisions that you make. Your future will be shaped by the decisions that you make. If you are going to shape your future, why not shape a good one?

I am going to spend a few minutes today reflecting on the things I am doing well, and I am also going to devote a little time to drafting a plan on how to fix the things that are not going so well. I encourage you to do the same.

#12: Note that there is value in not pursuing some goals.

There are a lot of things I believe very strongly in. I believe that you have to maintain a healthy work life balance in order to experience true happiness at work and at home. I believe that you need to a set of goals that help you steer your life. I have professional goals and I have many personal goals.

Maybe you have goals related to a promotion you want, or an ideal weight you would like to be at, or how much money you would like to have in the bank. If you do have goals, and I hope that you do, I think it is important to take the time to write them down. Writing them down is the first step in creating an actual plan that will help you achieve your goals, but it also gives you an opportunity to see how all of the goals in your life fit together.

I honestly do not know many people that take the time to write down their goals. The few I do know that routinely write down their goals are some of the most successful people that I know. It has been my experience in life that there is a very strong correlation between those two things. I think writing down your goals is a great personal habit to develop, and I also believe that you have to take it a step further. You need to consider how all of your goals are related to one another.

I think most people tend to look at their goals in isolation. As a result, we develop plans to achieve those goals that have very little chance of success, because they conflict with other parts of our lives. I would love to compete in an Ironman Triathlon. The event is made up of a 2.4 mile swim, a 112 mile bike ride, and then finally a 26.2 mile run.

To simply finish one would be a goal worth pursuing, but it is not something that I am likely to do in the near future. For me, to realistically have a chance to complete the race would require about 20+ hours of training each week for an 8-10 month period. I could easily draft the plan to do it, but when I look at that goal in comparison to other goals that I have in my life, it just doesn't fit. It would throw my life completely out of balance, and I feel the stress that be generated would far outweigh any joy that completing the event would bring me. This is one of those things I am going to file away under someday. There are several other goals that I am pursuing now that I feel make better use of my time. My other goals also are a bit more in harmony with each other.

If you have a few moments today, think about your goals. Think about your fitness goals, your professional goals, your relationship goals, your financial goals, your spiritual goals, and whatever other types of goals you may have. Take a moment to write them down and think about how they relate to one another.

Sometimes you have to make tough decisions and postpone a goal that will not work in harmony with your other goals, but I think it is an extremely important exercise to help you maintain a healthy balance in your life.

#13: Deal with personnel problems immediately.

I had a friend that worked for the Busch Gardens amusement park in Tampa. She told me that employees there could be terminated if a manager witnessed them walking by litter on ground.

When I first heard, that it seemed a little extreme to me, but then I thought about it a little more. Many families will save up for a year or more for a family vacation. The expectations are high as the family sets off on that first day of vacation. They want a magical experience that takes them away from the realities of their day to day life. They come to amusement parks, like Busch Gardens, to escape reality.

When you first walk into Busch Gardens, you do feel like you have been transported to a magical land. The park is pristine, and the landscaping is impeccable. I can imagine that discarded soda bottles and other litter would take away from the magical perception that you get when you walk in.

I don't know if Busch Gardens actually does fire employees for walking past litter, but I understand the principle they are trying to enforce: Problems should be dealt with swiftly, by the first employee that encounters them.

It is a good philosophy for managers, too. It is important for managers to swiftly address any problems they encounter. If you are a manager, your employees have an expectation that you are going to be the problem solver for your team. When problems arise, you cannot bury your head in the sand. You have to be the leader and address issues, head on.

Squabbles between employees, attendance issues, performance issues, and feuds between departments are just a few of the issues that need to be dealt with promptly. If you do not deal with these types of issues, there are a number of things, such as the following, that are likely to occur:

1. The problem will get bigger.

If you allow employees to come in ten minutes late without saying a word, eventually someone is going to starting coming in 20 minutes late, then 30 minutes late... Where do we draw the line? Who has to pick up the slack when employees come in late? I will tell you who does: the employees that were conscientious enough to come in on time. How do you think they are going to feel about you not addressing tardiness issues with some team members?

2. *You will not be a leader.*

In order to be a leader, you must have followers. If your employees start to sense you are not going to do anything to solve problems, they will start taking their problems to someone else—maybe to your manager or to another department's manager. When this occurs, you are a leader in title only, and your employees will jump ship at the first opportunity they can find to get off your team.

3. *Morale will stink on your team.*

When managers overlook important issues, morale starts to quickly drop. Low morale leads to high turnover. High turnover leads to much higher training costs and much lower productivity. Higher costs, high turnover, and poor morale lead to a new manager.

It can be intimidating to jump into a situation and have an uncomfortable conversation with one of your employees, but I assure you that procrastination is only going to make the problem worse.

#14: Assess if your home page is killing your productivity.

It is easy to waste a great deal of time online. I can't tell you how many hours I have lost by clicking on Twitter for "just a minute." A tweet will catch my eye that leads to me reading an article which leads me to another article. Then I remember why I was getting on Twitter in the first place. I go back, and yet another tweet will catch my eye and the cycle repeats itself.

I am picking on Twitter, but the same process holds true for reading blogs or even the newspaper. There are times, like an easy Sunday morning, where that may not be a problem, but there are other times when I need to be focused on things I have to do.

One of the tricks I have found to reduce my chances of being distracted is to change the home page on my internet browser to something that is not likely to distract me. I used to have the Google news page as my home page—one of the worst ideas I ever had. Every single time I logged on to the internet, I was immediately face-to-face with twenty of the day's top news stories. I couldn't help myself. I would always click on one or two of them. Sure, I only lost ten minutes or so, but when you do that several times a day, the time really starts to add up.

An easy fix would be to not go on the internet, but that is not a viable solution for me. My job does require me to be on the internet from time to time, so I had to find a way to log on without losing my focus. I changed my home page to the generic Google search page. There are no articles on the page, nor is there anything else that might distract me in any way.

It may sound silly that a focused and driven gentleman such as me has to remove these petty distractions in order to not lose valuable time in my day, but I do. I think most people are easily distracted.

Do you find yourself wandering the internet sometimes during your workday? Is surfing the net really the most important thing that you could be doing at that moment? If I ask you to prioritize everything you need to do for the day, where would surfing the net fall on your list?

My message is very simple. If you want to help maximize your chances of being more productive, change your browser's home page to something that is not likely to distract you. I recommend the Google search page, but I am sure that there are other plain vanilla sites out there as well.

Is your home page distracting you? It is an easy fix. Change it, and change it now.

HOW TO MANAGE PEOPLE BETTER

None of us are born managers. There is no management gene that we get from our parents. It is a learned skill. No matter what point of your career you are at, I can assure you there is more to learn.

Managing people is a very complex science. There is no formula I can provide you that will work with everyone, all the time. People are very complex and therefore you will need a variety of approaches to be truly effective as a manager. On the following pages, you will find a number of tips and tricks I have learned over the years. Figure out which ones may work for you and your situation.

#15: Understand that criticism can be good for you.

Nobody likes to be criticized. I do not deal well with criticism. I can be defensive. In fact, I would argue that everyone can be a little defensive at times. I am slowly learning not to immediately go into defensive mode when someone dares to criticize my work. I am also learning not to attack the messenger when criticism is offered.

Defensiveness has not served me well. At times during my career, it has helped me to build teams where no one would dare speak against my ideas. This, in turn, has led to some pretty stupid ideas being implemented, only to fail miserably. Are you getting honest criticism from your team? Are you sure?

How are we supposed to behave when faced with criticism? Not sure I know the exact answer to that, but I can tell you what I have done lately that seems to be working. When one of my team members offers up a dose of constructive criticism, the first thing I do is listen. It is harder than it sounds.

Upon hearing criticism, I think most people instantly start thinking about why the speaker is incorrect. At that point, you have stopped listening and started preparing your defense. You may be missing the point of their criticism. Try to clear your mind and listen.

When they are done, the first thing you should do is thank them for having the courage to speak up, and then assure them you will think about what they had to say, whether you agree with it or not. You should then take a while and consider what they had to say. Is there anything you can learn from their critique? Is there anything you can or should do differently?

I have to go out of my way to make sure I appreciate the people that are criticizing me, but I do need to appreciate them, because they are making me a better manager and perhaps a better person.

So, how well do you take criticism?

#16: Know that performance reviews count.

Most organizations conduct annual performance reviews of their employees, and in many cases the annual performance review is tied to salary increases. In other words, the annual performance review impacts the employee's ability to provide for their family. It is by far one of the most important things a manger is responsible for. So why is it that so many managers have a difficult time writing and delivering those annual performance reviews? It is because they treat it as an annual event as opposed to making it part of their daily or weekly routines.

When it is handled as an annual event, the many benefits of managing performance are lost. The annual review process does not have to be the meaningless waste of time that it is in many organizations. With just a little bit of preparation, it can be used to drive employee performance beyond your greatest expectations.

Is there a secret to improving work performance and making the annual review process almost effortless? Yes, there is. It starts with making sure managers and employees know what they must accomplish. When everyone understands what they are supposed to do, then it is much easier for them to contribute to the success of the organization. Productivity improves, and before you know it, you are starting to manage proactively instead of reactively.

If you are only looking at the goals on your performance appraisal once a year, you are looking at them in hindsight. Once the year is over, it is too late to affect the outcome. If you want to successfully achieve your goals, it takes a daily focus. Knowing where you are each day and making adjustments will be the key to your success.

Let me give you a simple example: Let's say I wanted to save $1,000 next year. Most people would look for ways they could come up with the $1,000 by making one adjustment in their life such as hitting the lottery, but if you break that goal down, it becomes much more achievable. $1,000, divided by the 365 days in the year, breaks down to saving $2.74 a day. Suddenly saving $1,000 seems like a very achievable goal. Surely I can save $2.74 a day. That's not even the price of a cup of coffee. I could then set up checkpoints for myself at the end of each week.

At the end of each week, I would ensure that I have saved $19.18. If I come up a little short one week, then I know I have to save a little extra the next week. By assigning weekly checkpoints and adjusting my plans for the next week based on the previous week's results, I greatly increase my chances of hitting my goal. Even if I come up a little short at the end of the year, I will have likely gotten far closer to my goal by following this process than if I simply waited to win the lottery.

Setting goals for your employees is no different. If the only time goals are reviewed is at the annual review, then it is already too late. Reviewing their progress against their goals throughout the year lets them know that the goal is important to you and also gives them a chance to make adjustments that will increase the likelihood they will hit their goals. The goals are the key to the entire appraisal process.

#17: Create a vision for your employees.

I have heard a lot of people talk about leaders needing vision. While I appreciate a good theoretical conversation, I thought I might put out a little more practical advice on this topic.

I agree that a successful manager has to create a compelling vision for their employees. In a nutshell, your employees need to know how the company is doing, where the company is headed, and what they specifically can do to help it to be successful. You need to create a vision of the future that inspires employees and compels them to perform at their best.

Ask yourself the following questions:

- Do your employees know the goals of the company?
- Do they know the goals of your department?
- Do they know what they specifically need to do in order for the company to succeed?

If you think they know the answers to all of these questions, I challenge you to go ask your employees. See if their answers match up to what you think they should be.

Take some time today to share your vision with your employees, but give them a sense of purpose and a reason to care. Put yourself in their shoes. What would inspire you?

#18: Step away from your keyboard (every now and then).

I am a big fan of working alongside my employees. I like to jump into the trenches and perform all of the job functions that I am responsible for overseeing. I don't necessarily do it every day; in fact, I can't even say that I do it every week. I have a full-time job with full-time responsibilities, but I do periodically make some time to work alongside my employees.

The reason I take the time to perform the job functions for which I am responsible is that I find it provides me several key benefits, such as the following:

1. Firsthand Knowledge

When I am working alongside my team, I can see firsthand the impact of the policies and procedures we have in our department. I can see if they make sense and if the employees are even aware of them. If the policies are not being followed, it is a good chance to investigate why. Was the policy not communicated, does it just not make sense, or is it a policy we even need? It also gives me a chance to see what challenges and obstacles my team is facing every day.

Sometimes people can get used to a problem, and they stop trying to get it fixed. They just live with it.

I recently found an employee who had an outdated computer that was not performing at the level she needed to effectively do her job. Why hadn't anyone addressed this? Probably because it had been a problem for so long that she just learned to live with it. These are the kinds of obstacles that you uncover.

2. Morale Building

Everyone wants to believe their boss has an understanding of what they do. I know what my employees do, because I have done it. Amazing things can happen when your employees believe you understand their jobs. They are much more likely to come forward with complaints, concerns, or suggestions. When you are communicating, everyone tends to be happier. Ideas get implemented, and morale skyrockets.

3. *Help with Managing*

I hate when I sit in meetings with other managers, and they can not answer the simplest questions about what their team does. I know my processes backwards and forwards.

When I am in meetings, I do not make commitments that my team has no shot at achieving. Folks tend to think I am a lot brighter than I am because I can speak in great detail about everything I am responsible for. It just requires that I periodically spend a little time with my team, doing what they do and seeing everything through their eyes.

Fight the urge to sit in your office all day answering email. Step away from your keyboard; get out there; and walk a mile in the shoes of one of your employees. I promise you good things will come from it.

Has anyone ever have a boss that had no understanding of what your job actually entailed? What did that do for the team's morale?

#19: Respect your interviewing karma.

If you are reading this I assume you are already in a management position or you aspire to be in a management position. A manager is a person with great power and, as we all know from Spiderman, "With great power comes great responsibility."

Most mangers will, on occasion, have the opportunity to interview job applicants, in the hope of filling an open position. It is important to empathize with the applicant. I know there have been times in my life I was desperate to get a job. Seeking a job can be a very humiliating and painful process for job applicants. Always keep that in mind. Go out of your way to ensure you are fully engaged with the applicant, and remain polite and attentive, even when you have determined they are not going to be a good fit for your organization.

I have helped a lot of job applicants to get a job. Many of those jobs were not my department, or even my company. I do a lot of networking, and if I know of an opportunity that would be a better fit for an applicant, I steer them in that direction by making the appropriate introduction.

How appreciative do you think those folks have been? Do you think they would be likely to help me if they were ever in a position to do so?

Be nice. It is a good rule to follow for conducting interviews and for conducting your life.

#20: Network better.

One of the skills I intend to develop further this year is my ability to network. Throughout my career I have traditionally not been a good networker. I am certainly not an introvert; I just have never put any effort into networking. To help me prepare to become a better networker, I have reached out to many of my friends and colleagues to determine how they are able to successfully build massive networks within their industries. They gave me a lot of tips, which will be in a later section of this book. They also gave me a few examples of networking errors.

Since I am more familiar with the errors, I have elected to write about those here.

1. Need-Based Contact

I listed this first because it is probably the most applicable to me. I am very busy on most days, so it is very rare that I reach out to someone just to say hello and to see how they are doing. This is the key to networking, in my opinion.

Think about it in terms of your friends. If you have several close friends you keep in regular contact with, wouldn't you go out of your way to help them if you were in a position to do so? What if you had a "friend" that you only heard from when they needed something, such as help moving, a ride to the airport at 3:30 a.m., or money? Would you be as likely to help that person? Professional networking is no different.

Don't let the first time you reach out to someone in months or years be because you need something. Benjamin Franklin was quoted as saying "The time to fix the roof is when the sun is shining." The same concept holds true in networking, the time to build your network is when you do not need anything. You can't fix the roof during a hurricane, and you can't build your network if you only maintain contact when you want something.

I have now carved out 15 minutes each week that I will use purely for maintaining or expanding my network. You may not need to be that structured, but I need to have a definitive plan if I am going to make anything happen.

2. Not Following-Up

Traditionally, after meeting new people and exchanging business cards, I forget totally about that person and throw their business card into the bottom of my laptop bag. That was 2012 me.

This year for me is going to be a lot more proactive about sending a follow-up note to my new contacts. Within 24 hours of making a new contact, I will shoot them a quick email to let them know how nice it was to meet them, and I will also follow up on any open-ended items that we might have discussed.

This note will take me less than two minutes to craft, and will help me stand out to the other person. I am sure they meet a lot of people each year that they barely remember, but sending a quick note greatly increases my chances of being remembered. It also ensures they have my contact information. I am much more likely to put someone into my outlook contacts from an email rather than their business card. With one click, I can add them to my outlook contacts as opposed to having to enter all of their information.

3. Not Asking Questions

Asking questions is a good networking technique. (It also works well when dating.) People generally like to talk about themselves. They want to tell you about their jobs, their kids, their lives, etc. Let them. Aside from identifying some common ground you might be able to build a relationship from, it allows the speaker a chance to talk about their favorite topic.

Giving the other person an opportunity to talk about themselves, while you are actively listening, significantly increases the chances that they will leave the conversation with a favorable opinion of you.

4. Being Too Pushy

When attempting to network in a face-to-face setting, you must be able to read the verbal and non-verbal cues the other person is sending you.

Sometimes people are just not in a "networking" mood, and you have to live with that. If the guy sitting next to you on the plane does not look up from his book while you are talking to him, take the hint, and stop talking. Likewise, if someone is constantly looking around while talking to you, thank them for their time, and let them go wherever it is they want to get to. Letting them get away is far better than holding them against their will.

5. *Seeking a Problem Solver*

Several of the greatest networkers that I know have told me you should never just send your resume to your contacts and ask them to forward it to anyone that might be interested. They, instead, have advised to seek advice from those contacts. Let them know that you are at a crossroad in your career and you are seeking advice on how to proceed. Based on their knowledge and experience, you felt they might be best suited to provide you that advice.

Now, instead of just asking them to do something, you have put them on a pedestal and let them know you have a great deal of respect for them. If they know of any opportunities that might be right for you, I am confident they will let you know and will eagerly help you make the right connection. Plus, who knows, you may actually get some good career advice you can use.

I have never done this, but this seems like a pretty intelligent approach to me.

#21: Note that fortune favors the bold.

Most men, in general, don't like to dance. For example, back in their school days, young men are socially contracted to attend school dances; however, you still tend to see a lot of guys hiding in the corners and clinging to the walls. The few brave souls that do venture out onto the dance floor are usually rewarded with the undivided attention of many young ladies seeking a dance partner.

That gentleman holding up the wallpaper will spend a lifetime thinking about what might have happened if they had ventured onto the dance floor.

There is a Latin proverb that claims, "Fortune favors the bold." In other words, good things happen to those willing to take risks.

Fortune favors the bold in business as well. I know there are a lot of aspiring managers reading this book. Good for you! Learning as much as you can about the art of management is certainly a step in the right direction, but I am going to give you advice that will help you more than anything else I have said here: ***Make an effort to be visible to management.***

Don't hold up the wallpaper. I have talked with many employees that have stated, "I don't think my manager even knows who I am or what I do." If you feel this way, it is up to you to correct the situation. If you are serious about moving ahead, you have to ensure people know who you are.

I pull my whole team together at least once a month and deliver a "State of the Union"-type address. I let everyone know how the company is doing, how our particular business unit is doing, and anything else I think they may need or want to know.

At the end, I always ask for questions. I have two or three employees I can count on to ask a question, but the overwhelming majority of folks will never ask anything. This is a golden opportunity for someone to speak up and get the attention of my entire management team, but very few take advantage of the opportunity.

The last thing I do is invite everyone to stop by my office should they think of any questions later. No one ever stops by. Even if you are too shy to speak in front of the group, take advantage of "open door" policies.

Talk to your managers. Talk to managers from other departments. Don't spend the rest of your day, week, or life thinking about the opportunities you missed. Be visible.

When the opportunity presents itself, I hope you dance!

#22: Focus on people.

As a manager, it is easy to get caught up in the tasks your team needs to accomplish each day. You're tracking productivity and checking things off your to-do list. For most new managers, this is right in their comfort zone. Before they became a manager, they were an employee that was likely very good at knocking out various tasks.

There is nothing wrong with tracking productivity and crossing things off your to-do list. I do these things myself. As a manager, it is important to remember that your primary objective is to help your employees work more effectively. In other words, how can you help them to get more tasks completed satisfactorily?

One thing you want to do is to match the right person to the right job. If you have someone that hates being on the phone, try to avoid keeping them in a job that requires a lot of phone work. Is there another function in your office they may be able to do in which they would be more efficient? If there is not another function, is there anything you can do to help them to be a little more efficient in their current position? Can you help them with training, coaching, or even just listening to their concerns?

Every employee wants something out of their job. If you can help them determine what that is and help them to get it, you will find that many more tasks are getting done with greater efficiency. Yes, your job is about getting tasks completed, but you accomplish that by putting your people into a position where they can excel.

#23: Build accountability.

When I come across organizations, departments, or teams that are struggling to perform at an acceptable level, there is one trait they almost always share and that is lack of accountability. It will destroy the efficiency and productivity of any team. A leader has to communicate a vision and direction to their team. They also have to establish goals and objectives. All of that activity is worthless if there is no accountability in the process.

So how can we build a little accountability into those that we lead? The following are some ways:

1. Be specific.

An ambiguous vision leads to ambiguous results. A leader must clearly and confidently set the course. What is it the team/organization is trying to accomplish? How exactly are we defining success? Along the way, how can team members know if they are on course or not? The more specific you are in establishing your success criteria, the more likely your team will be successful.

2. Don't be that specific.

As a leader, it is your job to create a vision and establish goals. Don't tell your team how to accomplish those goals. When you start dictating every step they are to make, they no longer feel like they have any part in the process at all. If it is your plan and your execution, they feel no ownership.

If you want employees to feel some level of accountability, you have to give them some power to influence the outcome. Let them determine how to achieve objectives. Give them clear goals, but also give them a lot of latitude around how to achieve those goals.

3. Recognize those that take responsibility.

Make sure you take a moment to acknowledge those that step up and take ownership of problems and accept their accountability. Their decisions may not be perfect, but if they own them, I think that is worth a pat on back. Recognize and reward the behaviors you want to see.

4. Model accountability.

I am not afraid to tell you when I completely screwed something up. I will share my logic and ask for forgiveness, but I am accountable for my results. I try very hard to not point fingers when things go bad. Instead, I look at my own actions to see what I could have done differently to produce a different outcome.

If you want anyone under you to be accountable for anything, you are going to have to be accountable yourself. It sounds easy as I write this, but I know personal accountability is a hard concept to master. I am not claiming to have mastered it. I have good days and bad, like most of you, I suspect.

5. Remember to hold them accountable.

When you establish goals for your team, there is usually a deadline associated with them. When that date comes around, you have to hold your team accountable. If they hit their objectives, shower them with praise rewards, and if they did not, it is time to have some difficult conversations.

Why did the team fail to hit the objectives? What changes are you, the leader, going to make in order to increase the team's chances of success on their next objective?

#24: Build an internal network.

I like to schedule everything. Not because I don't like spontaneity, but mainly so I don't forget anything. One of the things I schedule each week is fifteen minutes to send two notes. During the course of the week, I will engage with a lot of different people, some within my department and many outside of my department. Some of those interactions go smashingly well. People show up to meetings on time, prepared and they are fully engaged. We quickly solve the problem at hand and go back to our normal routines.

It would be very easy to take those positive interactions for granted. I think it is human nature to focus on the negative. So when meetings don't go well and people don't do their jobs, we tend to contact their supervisors, send nasty notes, or develop workarounds. I never forget to do those things. What I do tend to forget are all of those positive interactions I have each week.

So I schedule fifteen minutes each week to focus on two of those positive interactions. I try and recall at least one person in my department that I think had an excellent week. I send them a quick note to acknowledge their efforts, to encourage them to keep being excellent, and to express my sincere gratitude.

The second note I send each week, goes to someone outside of my department. Each week, I interact with folks from accounting, HR, facilities, IT, and various other groups that are well outside of my direct control. It is imperative that I maintain a successful relationship with each of these departments. My success depends on their support. So, once a week, I acknowledge someone outside of my department. I send them a note acknowledging all that they do, encouraging them to keep being excellent, and expressing my gratitude for their efforts.

I know for a fact that these notes have a huge impact on the recipients. These are the key players in the organization. They are the up and comers. These are the leaders of tomorrow. I want them on my side. Whether they stay with my company or move on to positions in other companies, they are going to remember me fondly. They will remember me because no one else is sending them notes, acknowledging their efforts.

The networking and strong relationships I build are not the reasons I send the notes. I send the notes because I am genuinely appreciative of whatever they have done to make the organization better.

Who can you send a note to? Who helped you last week? Whether that help was big or small, positive reinforcement is the best tool you have for influencing the behavior of others. It is also very convenient that it is the right thing to do.

How do you recognize the little positive things people do each week?

#25: Give your employees a reason to have faith in you.

There are a lot of things a leader has to do to be successful. One of the most important and often overlooked things is to develop a sense of responsibility among your subordinates. Let's change that to "develop a sense of responsibility among your employees." I don't like the word "subordinates." It has a negative connotation to it, or maybe that's just how I take it. I don't want to be anyone's subordinate, but I am happy to be an employee. I digress...

I work with a lot of managers that feel the need to check their emails and call in several times, whenever they take a day off or go on vacation. I truly think some of them do it because they think it makes them appear like a better manager. They must be important if they can't take a day off. This is not a philosophy I subscribe to.

If you manage a group of people, and you have been managing them for more than ninety days, there is something very wrong if you can't take a day off without checking in several times.

Your people have to be empowered to make decisions and carry on in your absence. If you do not have enough faith in their abilities, you either need to spend some time developing those abilities or get some new people.

One way to develop those skills is to share your logic on the decisions that you make. Whenever I make a big decision, I try to ensure that my team understands the thought process I went through to come to that decision. I do this for the following two reasons:

1. *I may be making the wrong decision.*

If there is a flaw in my logic, I know my team will point it out. This helps me improve my decision making skills.

2. *They learn what factors they need to consider.*

Once they understand the points I take into consideration, they can use that same logic to make similar decisions in the future. Even if I end up being wrong, we can all determine where the logic was flawed and learn from my mistake.

The side benefit of sharing the logic you use on a regular basis is that it helps your employees to build up faith and confidence in you. Whenever decisions get made, employees can come up with some pretty crazy ideas on why the decision was made.

I cancelled our holiday party a couple of years ago. In the industry that I am in, December is always a very bad month for us. This had been a particularly bad year, and December was unusually slow for us. We had people working reduced hours, and I was trying my hardest to keep them employed. I did not feel it was in their best interest to spend a couple of thousand dollars on a holiday party.

I announced that we were going to cancel the party, but I failed to explain the reason why in sufficient detail. As a result, the rumors started flying—everything from I would personally get a bonus for not spending the money (I assure you I did not) to the company was going to shut down our location, as the other locations had their Christmas parties.

I was a little irritated by all of this, so I pulled everyone together for a second time. I explained the logic in great detail. Once the logic was shared, everyone was completely on board. As a matter of fact, several employees have questioned the need to have our holiday parties in subsequent years.

When decisions get made behind closed doors and changes are made with no explanation, bad things happen. When no information is provided, rumors start and spread like wildfire. The cure for this is to provide your logic up front. If you share the logic you use on a regular basis, you will find your employees will have much more faith in you as a leader, and they will learn to use the same logic in their decisions.

When they start to use the same logic in their decisions, you can stop checking in on your day off because you will have more faith in them. If you are uncomfortable sharing the logic you are using on a decisions, you really need to rethink the decision.

Have you ever worked for someone that made decisions behind closed doors? Did you always assume they were making decisions that were in your best interest?

#26: Offer sincere apologies when appropriate.

One thing they did not teach in graduate school was how to issue an apology. Over the course of my twenty year career, I have had a lot of opportunities to apologize. On some occasions I have issued sincere heartfelt apologies that have helped to cement solid personal and professional relationships. Other times, the apologies were not as sincere and may have done more harm than good.

Apologies are an important tool for managers. We are never going to be perfect communicators. We are never going to react correctly to every situation. Apologies are important because they mend relationships. Given a little time, I think most people are capable of forgiveness and can move past almost anything. I think apologies speed up the forgiveness process.

I think the most important thing an apology does is let the recipient know they matter. If you lose your cool with someone and then pretend like it never happened, I think that you send a very strong message that their opinion does not matter to you. Failing to apologize may not only impact your relationship with the person you have wronged. People talk. Word of your transgressions will spread and others will start to form opinions that may not be accurate. Effective apologies can communicate you are aware of the transgression and it is not likely to be repeated.

I think many times we are too embarrassed to offer an apology. We start to rationalize that our wrongdoing was not a big deal. We might even try to convince ourselves we did nothing wrong at all, or we may attempt to transfer the blame to the victim. "They got what they deserved because they were being unreasonable."

Learn to recognize these behaviors in yourself. I am very good at transferring the blame to the victim. It is one of my strong points. I have learned over time to recognize this behavior. When I start to do it, alarm bells in my head start to go off, and I try to take another look at the situation.

So, how do you go about apologizing once you recognize you need to? There are three major components to the apology:

1. *Acknowledgement*

You have to admit you were wrong. The apology is pretty weak without this component. Many politicians and celebrities have tried to make apologies without acknowledging any wrongdoing. If you are apologizing because you are truly sorry, acknowledgement has to be a part of it.

2. *Regret*

If you are acknowledging you did indeed do something wrong, the next logical step is you will want to express some regret. For example, "I regret the way I handled that," or "I know I should not have spoken to you like that."

3. *Assurance*

You need to be able to assure the recipient the offensive action will not be repeated. If you truly felt you did something wrong and you do honestly regret it, I hope you would not want to commit the same offence in the future. Assure the recipient that you have learned from your transgression.

There are a couple of things that I suggest you not do when apologizing. The first is using the phrase, "I want to apologize." What does that mean? *Are* you apologizing? Or do you simply wish you could but have determined you are not capable? "I want to apologize" is not an apology. Speaking of verbiage, don't get cute with your selection of words—such as, "I'm sorry you feel that way." Be direct, and use simple words.

#27: Stop rewarding bad behavior.

I have never met a manager that at some point has not rewarded bad behavior. We all do it. Have you ever worked for a company that did an across the board pay raise for all employees? Everybody gets a 2% raise or something along those lines? I have seen it more than once. It is insulting to the people that work hard, and it rewards those that do not pull their weight. It encourages laziness, because it is the laziest form of management. It tells each worker you do not care enough about them to actually evaluate their performance.

When I was climbing the corporate ladder, I was forced to roll out across the board pay raises at several different points. I am fortunate enough now to work at a company I do not believe would ever condone such behavior.

At this point in my life, I don't think I would ever again go along with this type of policy. It undermines good management, and I will never stand for it again.

Across-the-board pay raises are not the only way we reward bad behavior. We fail to address the employee that comes in late every day. It is only a couple of minutes, right? If I come in ten minutes late each day, I will work 43 hours less a year than my counterparts who come in on time. The tardy employee is essentially rewarded with a week's paid vacation each year. Not only that, but do you think they will limit it to ten minutes?

If I come in ten minutes late and you fail to address it, I will not think twice about hitting the snooze button tomorrow and coming in fifteen minutes late.

How do you dole out the work that needs to be done each day? Do you give the hardest projects to your laziest employees? Of course not, you give the hardest work to your best employees because they can handle it. You give the simple and easy stuff to the slackers. For being lazy, they are rewarded with easier work. What lesson are they learning?

I know why we do it. Our instincts tell us to give the hard stuff to the talented people because they will knock it out with minimal questions and we know they will hit their deadlines. It is easier for the manager to give the hard stuff to the best employees. That's okay to do every now and then, but if you do it consistently, it starts to send a very bad message. The harder you work, the more work I am going to give you.

Chances are that you are not going to make it up to them at evaluation time. They may get a higher score on their evaluation, but financially, is it really going to make a difference?

Most companies are in the 2-3% range for increases, if you are lucky. If I have two managers that make $30K a year and one is a superstar and one is a slightly below average performer, chances are that their increases will not be significantly different. Say Manager A gets a 4% raise, and Manager B gets a 2% raise. Their salaries are now $31,200 and $30,600 respectively. It is a difference of about $11 in pay a week. That is hardly punishing bad behavior.

So what are we as managers to do?

1. *Address bad behavior immediately when you see it.*

If you see it, so do all of your employees. If you do nothing, their faith in you as a leader will erode over time. It also sends a clear message that bad behavior will be tolerated, which in turn encourages more bad behavior.

2. *Reward good behavior.*

Does your company have a perfect attendance award? How valuable is an employee you know is going to show up for work each and every day? Pretty valuable in this day and age, yet most companies do not reward perfect attendance. Rewards do not have to be financial, although money is nice too. Each quarter, all of my managers chip in, and we give $100.00 to the employee we feel had the best performance. It is not much, but I truly believe that it means a heck of a lot to the winners.

3. *Stop giving increases to employees that are not meeting the minimum standards.*

It is harsh I know, but if you are going to succeed as a company, you have got to encourage employees to either meet the standards or move on.

#28: Learn how to manage remote employees.

My company has several operations centers scattered across the globe. This means that I have responsibilities for employees that work remotely from my location. Managing remote employees is a real challenge. Training and communication become exponentially harder, but I have figured out a few tricks to managing remote employees that I would like to share with you now.

1. *Selecting the right employees is crucial.*

Selecting the right person for an open job is critical for any manager, but it is even more critical when you are going to fill a position that will be remote. Communication is the key, and if someone is not a good communicator, you may be setting yourself up for failure if you hire them. These are definitely positions I would use multiple interviewers for.

2. Availability and expectations need to be crystal clear.

What hours are you expecting your employee to be available? Nail this down and make sure that both of you are clear.

I have seen this issue create a lot of frustration on both sides. Also, what hours will you be available? If you are in a different time zone, you need to let your employees know when it is okay to call. If you really don't mind them calling during off hours, you need to let them know, or you need to let them know what they should do if you don't want them to call.

3. Conduct face-to-face meetings.

When you are starting to build a new relationship with a remote employee, you want to start the relationship by spending a little bit of time face to face. If your travel budget allows for this, it can pay huge dividends. Face-to-face meetings are the key to establishing successful long-term remote relationships.

After the initial meeting, I would recommend at least quarterly face-to-face meetings after that.

4. Have consistent employee meetings.

I have written previously on the value of conducting one-on-one meetings each week, with all of your direct reports. If you have remote employees, this is a mandatory practice, in my opinion. Schedule a little time each week you can go over their goals and the progress they have made against them.

This is also their chance to present any problems they have encountered or concerns they want you to know about. These meetings are essential to building an effective relationship with your remote employees.

5. Establish a feedback loop.

Periodically ask yourself if you are getting everything you need from your remote employees. Determine if you are communicating enough or whether you need to establish new ways to communicate more. Get feedback from them. See what their frustrations are. Analyze what is working well, what is not working well, and what you can do to correct it.

#29: Don't be a micromanager.

Could you be a micromanager? Before you answer that, consider how many people you have met who have readily admitted to being a micromanager. I have never met anyone that admitted they were, but I have met many people that have claimed their boss is a micromanager.

There is a big disconnect there that leads me to believe we are not very good at recognizing micromanagement in ourselves. The mere mention of the word micromanager makes me cringe, as I have had some bad experiences.

So how do you know if you are a micromanager? Here are some clues.

1. You resist delegating tasks. You hand out the easy, boring or dirty tasks, but generally handle all of the important stuff yourself.
2. When you do delegate, you provide step-by-step instructions and hover over people as they are working.
3. You fault employees that do not follow the step-by-step directions regardless of the outcome of the process.
4. You tend to take back delegated work at the first sign of trouble.
5. You insist on employees consulting you whenever decisions need to be made.
6. You tend to work on your days off.
7. You have higher than normal turnover on your team.

There may be situations where micromanagement is the appropriate action, but in most cases, it tends to demoralize employees. Most people appreciate a little autonomy and look forward to showing off their decision making skills. You give them an objective, and they will amaze you with how creatively and competently they can complete it.

Aside from killing the morale of your employees, micromanagement also creates a workforce that is afraid to make a decision. It will generally slow down all of your processes as employees will wait for direction whenever an issue arises. Everyone becomes timid and tentative. The micromanager's ego tends to grow more every time they take a day off. When decisions can't get made without the manager, employees have no choice but to call their manager constantly when they are out of the office. Does this describe your situation?

If you suspect that you may be a micromanager, today is the day you can start to make a positive change. It will not be as difficult as you might think.

Here are the step-by-step instructions.

1. Give your employees assignments, not instructions.

Stop telling them how to do things. Just let them know what the goal is, when the deadline is, and any pertinent information they may need to know.

2. Give them confidence.

Let them know that you have faith in them and that is why you picked them for the assignment.

3. Leave the door open for communication.

Assure your employees you are here for them if they come up against an obstacle. Let them know your door is open if they need to brainstorm or just bounce ideas off of you. Put the invitation out there, but don't be offended if they don't take advantage of it, especially initially.

4. Provide checkpoints.

Let them know when you would like to receive updates on how the project is coming. Let them know how often and how much detail should be in their updates. Here is a hint: They should not spend more time updating you then they are spending working on the actual project.

5. Coach any failures.

It is possible that your employees may fail to accomplish the desired goal in the allotted time. This does not validate the need for you to personally oversee every detail; it simply means you have an opportunity to mentor someone. Conduct an after action review of the project. Talk about what went right, and what could be improved. Help them to find the error of the way. The lesson is much more meaningful if they can discover their own errors and determine how they could do it differently next time.

6. Recognize success.

When your employees successfully complete projects, make sure you take the time to acknowledge those efforts.

#30: Be accountable.

I do not think fondly of people that do not accept personal accountability. I think people that do accept personal responsibility have stronger relationships, provide more value to their organizations, and are much more respected by their peers.

If that is the case, why don't more people embrace the concept of personal accountability? I think we have been brainwashed by politicians, CEO's, and a host of other celebrities into thinking it's better to explain how it is not your fault than to accept responsibility for your actions.

I believe that effective leaders have to be masters at accepting personal accountability. When things go horribly wrong, deadlines are missed, or errors are made, leaders have to look inward to determine what they could have done differently to affect the outcome. I think this is a key characteristic a lot of leaders could benefit by developing, so I am going to give you three tips on how to develop this characteristic in your teams.

1. Set the expectation.

If you are a manager, you need to ensure your people understand excuses will not be tolerated. We cannot accept our employees pointing the finger of blame or explaining why it is not their fault.

I recently questioned an error that was made in my department and the response I got was the error was made by a brand new person. This did not sit well with me. As far as I know, we do not have a policy that encourages new employees to make errors. Our clients certainly are not going to care that it was a new employee that made the error.

I took it as an opportunity to help establish the manager's personal accountability. I asked what she could have done differently. What changes could she make to her training program to prevent this in the future? How could she have monitored the new employee more closely during the probationary period? I kept asking questions like this until I was quite confident she understood we were going to accept the accountability for this error.

2. *Provide consistent feedback.*

I meet with each of my direct reports one-on-one each week. This is my opportunity to review their progress against their goals and provide them feedback, both positive and constructive, on their performance over the course of the last week. This is the greatest opportunity I have to influence their behaviors. I praise them for taking accountability and personally owning issues that come up, and I help them to see the error of their ways when they are simply pointing fingers. This is the single greatest tool I have in my management arsenal.

If you are not conducting one-on-ones with your employees you should be.

3. *Lead by example.*

As a leader, you set the tone for your team. If you play the blame game every time an issue arises, you can count on your team members doing the same thing. The first person you need to take responsibility for is you.

When issues arise, ask questions like the following:

- What could I have done differently to prevent this issue?
- What training could I seek out to help prevent this type of issue?
- How could I have communicated more effectively in order to have prevented this issue?
- How can I make this situation right?

Sometimes instilling a little accountability can require some confrontational conversations, but in my opinion, it is a small price to pay. We need to stop worrying so much about looking good and focus a little more time and effort on actually being good.

#31: Promote from within, if it makes sense.

A new entry level management position opens up on your team, so do you promote from within or do you recruit from outside of your organization? Neither one of these answers will be right in every situation. Your goal should be to promote from within, but if your company is better served by bringing in outsider, you have to be prepared to do that.

For every open job I have ever been responsible for filling, I have always looked for applicants both inside and outside of the organization. I truly think this is the best practice. Even if you think you know exactly who you want to promote internally, I always think it is a good idea to see everyone available.

There are several things you can do to increase the likelihood you will be able to promote from within:

1. Hire the best people.

I have had a lot of managers tell me they did not hire someone because they felt they were overqualified. They assume the applicant will not stay for the long term.

This is not a philosophy I subscribe to. I will hire the best qualified applicant for any position. There is no way to guarantee any applicant will stay long term.

Hire the best and do your best to keep them engaged. If you hire the best people, it greatly increases the chances you will be able to promote from within at some point in the future.

2. Develop all of your employees.

I have a dedicated written plan on how I am going to develop particular skills for each one of my direct reports. I feel it is my responsibility as a manager to identify opportunities for them to learn new skills, or further enhance their current skills. I have to push them out of their comfort zones. If they don't like to speak in public I have to provide them the training and the opportunities to overcome that weakness. If they lack financial acumen, it is my responsibility to involve them in the budgeting process and ensure they understand the logic that goes into it.

Identifying what needs to be developed and drafting a plan to address it is one of the hardest things I have to do as a leader, but it has to be done. Do you have development plans for each of your employees?

3. Plan your succession.

If you get promoted tomorrow, who takes over for you? Instead spending a lot of time trying to figure out exactly who might take your place, try to prepare as many of your employees for advancement as you can. Taking a few minutes to think about what skills your employees will need to advance is time well spent, and it also will help with point #2.

If there are occasions you are unable to promote from within, make sure you note what skills your employees were lacking that kept them from being promoted. It then becomes your responsibility to address those shortcomings and ensure they are not passed over again.

Most people want to work in a place that offers some advancement opportunity. If you are repeatedly passing employees over for promotion, you cannot honestly have a reasonable expectation that they are going stay with your company.

When you promote from within, you get the advantage of having someone that already knows the company's culture and should be able to hit the ground the running. It also gives you flexibility in training their replacement. As they are not leaving the company, you still have them to help train the new hire that will replace them. This is a big advantage.

Like I said at the beginning of this section, there is no one right answer for every situation. I will say this: If you have been passed over for promotion several times and your manager has not adequately explained why, or taken the time to help further develop your skills, I think your chances of advancing in the future are not good.

Have a very frank conversation with your manager and ask them to explain exactly what you can do to be a more viable applicant for future opportunities. If you help push them into helping you develop your skills, great. If they dismiss you or refuse to even have the conversation, it is time to consider other options if you desire to advance.

#32: Develop your command presence.

I have a military background. I am grateful for the time I spent in the military, as I think it greatly helped to shape who I am today. One of the many things I learned in the military was command presence. For those of you not familiar with the term, it is the ability to walk into a room and convey a sense of confidence and competence to anyone you come in contact with. The people with command presence are deemed "natural leaders," because they are the ones that everyone else is going to for answers.

Sometimes, the people with command presence are the ones actually in charge, but in a lot of cases they may not have the title of manager or director. That does not mean they are not in charge.

Command presence is not a natural born ability. It is a culmination of learned behaviors. Do you have command presence? When you walk into a room, do people naturally assume you are in charge whether you are or not? If you feel you might be lacking in command presence, is there anything you can do to improve? My answer is "yes," and I am going to help you do it.

There are 3 steps I want you to focus on to improve your command presence, and they are the following:

1. *Appearance*

I am old school, so appearance is important to me. In order to convey a sense of competence to those that may not know you, it is important you do not look like you just crawled out of bed. I don't care what your office dress code is. Personally, I would shoot to dress better than my peers, but regardless of what dress code you go with, you want to present a neat appearance.

My clothes are clean, neat, and pressed every single day, without exception. My shoes are clean and shined. My hair is always neatly trimmed and styled. I get it cut every two weeks. I keep a change of clothes in my office, just in case I spill something on myself.

I am not saying you have to wear a suit and tie every day, but I am saying you must have a neat appearance. Rarely are people looking to the fellow wearing a wrinkled t-shirt, shorts, and flip-flips to lead them. Dress the part.

2. *Eye Contact*

Eye contact is very important if you are trying to develop your command presence. Leaders don't look at the floor. When you walk into a room and everyone glances up at you, your natural tendency is look down or look away. Don't do that. Look right back at them. Make eye contact with someone, hold it for a second, and move on to the next person.

When you are introduced to people, it is important to look them straight in the eye. In those first few moments of meeting someone, a lot of impressions are made that will have a bearing on your relationship with them.

Make a good impression by making eye contact. Even if you are intimidated, look them in the eye.

3. Speaking Up

When you speak, project your voice and speak slowly. Do you know anyone that tends to mumble when they get nervous? I know people like that, and they are not the ones I am looking to for leadership.

Speak in your voice, but do so confidently. The best way to perfect this is practice. Try it at home first. Focus on using the appropriate volume and saying each sentence with confidence. Get a loved one to critique you. I know it sounds silly, but practice makes perfect.

If you want to enhance your command presence, you need to master how to use your voice.

Essentially command presence is walking into a room like you own the place. Make sure your posture is good, your appearance is sharp, you are making good eye contact, and you are speaking confidently.

Observe the people around you today. Look for command presence. What do leaders do when they walk into a room that conveys a sense of competence and confidence? What subtle clues are there indicating they are in charge?

#33: Gather feedback from your employees before the exit interview.

Let's start with a definition. An exit interview is conducted by some companies when an employee has given their notice, but has not yet departed the company. The interviews are usually conducted by a Human Resources Manager, but sometimes they can be outsourced to third party companies.

During the interview, the departing employee is asked questions around the reasons they are leaving, what things the company does well, and what things the company needs to improve upon. The questions are usually pretty open ended and designed to let the employee talk about anything they feel strongly about. The thought process behind the exit interview is that is likely the most candid the employee will ever be, as they have nothing to lose by telling you the truth.

My background is in operations. I have always been in operations and likely always will. I have certainly hired and fired my share of people, but I have never worked in Human Resources. My thoughts are purely from an operational perspective. I am not an advocate of exit interviews. I think the theory that it is the point in time you are most likely to get candid response is dangerously flawed. What's in it for the employee? There is no way being candid on an exit interview will benefit them.

There are many employees that prove to be problematic for any number of reasons. As managers do their jobs effectively, these employees start to feel pressure to shape up or ship out. Many choose to ship out. These employees are going to use the exit interview as an opportunity to personally attack any of the effective managers that helped to drive them from the company. I do not like the idea of giving them a forum and an audience for their attack.

In the best case scenario, where you have a good employee that has worked in your organization for several years, I think the exit interview process is still flawed. When you quit your old job and you are about to embark upon a new one, you will start to find a lot of things you do not like with your old employer. Things that you tolerated for years will suddenly become intolerable. That old copier you have to kick to work right has now become a beacon of everything that is wrong with your old employer. The good employee is now going to rattle off a list of grievances in their exit interview they didn't know bothered them two weeks earlier. They are not being malicious; in fact, they are trying to give honest and sincere feedback. It is just very biased feedback, in my opinion.

The best time for an employee to discuss their concerns or suggestions is when they are committed employees with no desire to leave the organization. They are stakeholders at that point and I greatly value their opinions. This is when I want to solicit feedback from them.

I like to catch my new employees after they have gone through training and ask them how the on boarding process went. I get their feedback on how we can make training better and whether the company is living up to their expectations. My company does two or three internal employee surveys a year to elicit feedback on what we can do to make our company an even better place to work. A lot of good feedback has come from those surveys and a lot of suggestions have been implemented.

If your company uses exit interviews, and everyone, not just HR, is happy with the process you should absolutely continue that process. If you are getting good feedback and that feedback is being disseminated in a constructive manner, please email me and share how your process works.

If you are an employee and you are asked to participate in an exit interview, my advice is to not use it as a forum to list out every grievance you have ever had. If there has always been something that bothered you that you feel is a pretty important, share it. That is, if you have confidence that the interviewer is going to use the information constructively and get it into the right people's hands. If you don't have that confidence you may want to reconsider sharing anything.

I am an extremely vocal person. If I am unhappy, you will know it. I will give you every chance to right the things bothering me. If you choose not to, at some point, I will move on. When I do, don't expect me to list out my concerns yet again for you to ignore. I will just go away quietly.

That's my take on exit interviews. I realize this is a very controversial topic, so I hope all of you can at least respect my opinion, even if you disagree.

Have you ever been involved in an exit interview? If so, which side of the table were you on? Do you think they have value? Would you give your employer candid feedback in an exit interview? Why or why not?

#34: Learn the value of a notebook.

If you aspire to be in a leadership position, or even if you are already in a leadership position, I want to talk about the one piece of equipment you cannot do without. I am talking about a notebook. A notebook can help get you through bad times. It can help you to remember all of the little details that are otherwise forgotten in an instant. Most importantly, a notebook can take you to a whole new level of productivity. I love my notebook, and I would be lost without it.

My notebook is not fancy, probably because I am not fancy. I know a lot of executives carry moleskin notebooks or leather portfolios. I am not knocking anybody that does carry a moleskin notebook, but it is just not my style. I go with a standard three subject notebook like you would carry in middle school. It usually costs about a dollar.

Once you have decided on the style of notebook you are going to carry (did I mention you need to start carrying a notebook?), your next step is to use it effectively.

Here are a few of the ways that I use my notebook:

1. Meetings

In really good meetings, I use my notebook to jot down who attended and any action items that were assigned. In really bad meetings, where I am bored out of my mind, I use my notebook to make grocery lists or to jot down the things I need to get done on my next weekend break.

Nothing makes you look more involved in a meeting than taking notes. Whether those notes are at all related to the meeting, only you will know.

2. Moments of Brilliance

Occasionally I come up with a brilliant idea. If I don't write it down instantly, I forget it as soon as I see a shiny object. My mind goes in a dozen directions at one time. I need to write down any semi-intelligent ideas, or I will lose them forever.

If you want the secret to cranking out a good blog post on a more frequent basis, I would suggest carrying a notebook. Scribble down any half-baked idea you have. You can decide later whether it is worth pursuing, or not.

3. Communication

I have a 30 minute meeting with each of my direct reports each week. We discuss their progress against their goals, and anything either of us feels is relevant. I keep a running list for each one of them in my notebook. Instead of calling them into my office every time I have a thought, I just jot down the point and hit them all at once during their weekly meeting.

I also capture any action items for them, so we can follow up on them at a later point. I have a similar meeting with my boss. I also keep a running list for him. I appreciate that his time is valuable, so I use it efficiently by bundling my issues.

I also keep a running list of people I need to thank. This is something that should never slip my mind, but it does. I have dedicated time for sending thank you notes so that all I need to do is refer to my list at that time and no one is forgotten.

4. *Writing*

I am not sure at what point I can consider myself a writer, but I seem to be spending more and more time putting words on paper. There will be moments in the day I have a few minutes to kill. The meeting is supposed to start at 10:00, but does not actually start until 10:05 or 10:10. Instead of playing Angry Birds, I can use those five or ten minutes to write. I am cranking out 500-1000 words on my blog each day. I am writing twice that. Some of it I hold in reserve, and some of it doesn't make the cut. That's 2000 words a day.

I work 10 hours a day, commute for two hours, and try to get in at least an hour of working out. That does not leave me a whole lot of time for everything else, showering, meals, reading, or any other daily tasks. I need to take advantage of every minute. My trusty notebook allows me to do that.

At the end of each day, I review everything I wrote down. I put any new tasks or meetings into my calendar, as well as scheduling time to follow up on any of those brilliant ideas I might have had. I type any writing that I want to keep, and I also put any information that I want to file for later into Evernote.

Can you record all of these things electronically? Yes, but for me it never works out to be quite as efficient as using a pen and paper. Maybe I am old, but if you are recording all of these things electronically, and that system is working for you, don't change a thing.

I am fairly confident that people would think I was an idiot if not for my notebook. If you are not carrying a notebook, you have not begun to tap into your potential.

I beg you to get a notebook and give it a sincere try. I think that you will find that if you use it effectively it will make you a better leader, and perhaps a better person. It is a quick and easy way to Manage Better Now.

#35: Be careful with your open door policy.

Does your company have an open door policy? I think an open door policy sounds great, but in reality, it undermines the chain of command and creates levels of management that are incapable of thinking for themselves. That may sound overly harsh, but it is true. I would rather you hear it from me than to learn the lesson the hard way.

Most open door policies are not even policies. It is a phrase senior managers say to entry level employees. I think a lot of them say it because they think it is what the employees want to hear. Who knows, maybe it is what the employees want to hear. A true open door policy means any employee at any level can walk into any manager's office to discuss any issue at any time. Is that really what you want? Do you want Johnny from the mailroom plopping down in front of the CEO to discuss his frustration with the selection of soft drinks in the vending machine?

I am hoping the CEO has more important things to do. Things like generating new business, retaining existing clients, or developing strategic plans that will ensure I have a job for the next twenty years. That's what I want the CEO focused on.

A true open door policy can result in many levels of management being bypassed. It can undermine your entire chain of command. It allows for senior managers to look like problem solving heroes while making mid-level managers look like incompetent buffoons. It trains employees to bypass their manager and seek out the guidance of senior managers by rewarding them for this destructive behavior. They are rewarded by the senior manager listening to their issues and resolving their problems for them. This, in turn, teaches them to seek out the most senior person they can find whenever they have an issue. This is very destructive behavior for a company to engage in.

Senior managers end up being distracted from working on the things they should be working on, and mid-level managers become very frustrated, because their employees constantly go over their head, and will seek other employment if they have any sense. So why do we want to have an open door policy again?

The purpose is to make sure employees feel like they can discuss their problems with someone that will react to that discussion and seek to resolve the issue. The person they need to discuss their problems with needs to be their manager. The manager then needs the support and guidance of a senior manager to resolve the issue. This is how you develop problem solving managers.

No one on this planet is more of an advocate of communicating with employees at all levels than I am, but I do not have a traditional open door policy. Yes, any employee can come see me and talk about whatever their frustrations are, but I will cut them off very early in the conversation and ask if they have discussed it with their supervisor. If they have and they are still unhappy, I will hear them out and see if I can facilitate a more productive conversation with their supervisor. If they have not, I explain the merits of using the chain of command.

99% of the time they leave the office feeling empowered and ready to have that conversation with their supervisor. The other 1%? Well, some people are going to be unhappy regardless of what you do. They probably won't stay with you long.

Think about the repercussions of your actions. If you have managers that report to you, you cannot resolve the issues of their employees without first giving them an opportunity to resolve them. It is not just common courtesy; it is a good management practice and a great developmental opportunity.

#36: Build your empathy.

Lots of people have written that leaders need to be empathetic, but you can't tell somebody that and... Poof! They develop empathy. I guess the question is this: Can I teach someone to be empathetic? I am certainly going try, so here are my recommendations on how to develop your empathy.

1. Learn and use people's names.

I have mentioned this tip before, and I will very likely mention it again. Your employees are not nameless, faceless drones. They have names and probably lives outside of work, but we will get to that in a minute. Learn their names, and use them every time you see them.

This may sound simple, but I have seen managers make some fairly stupid personnel decisions because they did not know the names of their employees. It is harder to be mean to people and make arbitrary decisions about personnel cuts when you know people's names.

2. *Take an interest in people.*

You have things in common with all of your employees. Find out what those things are by communicating with them. Some days I sit down with my employees when they are in the break room and just ask them about their lives. We might talk about their kids, their spouse, their hopes, or their dreams. Mainly I just listen. I let them tell me whatever they want. I try to be an attentive listener, so that I can retain as much as possible. I try to learn their kids' names, or remember what their spouse does for a living.

This is time well invested, in my opinion. If you just listen you are going to become more empathetic along the way, whether you want to or not. The more you know about people, the harder it is to not care about them.

3. *Put yourself in their shoes.*

I can empathize with someone that is diagnosed with cancer. I can imagine how I would feel and the sort of things that would be going through my mind. I cannot feel their pain completely, but I can empathize if I really think about it. This is hard, because we all react to things a little differently, but for most of us, I think putting ourselves in their shoes helps us to know what to say and what not to say.

#37: Use LinkedIn to network effectively.

I have noticed something during the year or two I have been a member of LinkedIn. People tend to be the most active on the site when they want to leave their current job. That is certainly understandable, as it is a phenomenal tool for job seekers and recruiters alike, but I think it is a shame most people only use it when they need a job.

The real power of LinkedIn is networking. LinkedIn is a tool that makes it convenient for you to maintain all of the contact information for the many people that you have worked with over the years. It is a tool. That means it makes it easier to network, but it still requires you take a little initiative and put in some effort.

There are two things that I want you to do this weekend with LinkedIn that will make you a much better networker:

1. *Reach out.*

I have connections I have not spoken to in over ten years. If I suddenly lost my job tomorrow, how would it look if I suddenly reached out to them? It would look like I did not really care about them, but now that I need something I will take time out of my life to speak with them, to see if they can help me. That is not networking; that is using people when it is convenient for you.

I want you to spend a little time networking today. Find three of your contacts on LinkedIn that you have not spoken to in a while. Shoot each one of them a note. Ask them how they are doing, how their families are, and what is going on in their career. Let them know that you don't actually need anything, but you are just checking in to see how they are doing. How good would that make you feel if someone you knew 5-10 years ago just dropped you a note saying they were thinking of you and wanted to say hello? That would make me feel pretty good.

Spread a little joy today and reach out to some of those older contacts. It is always good to stay fresh in people's minds. That is how opportunities find you, even when you are not looking for them. Send three notes today, and keep sending three notes each weekend until you have reached out to all of your contacts.

2. *Find new contacts.*

LinkedIn does a great job of presenting other people you might know. Go through the list and make sure there is not anyone else you can add to your contacts. If you do find someone you should add to your contact list, take the time to send them a personal message.

When you hit the connect button, LinkedIn automatically gives you a standard message to send to your potential new contact. Do not use that message. If you truly want to connect with someone, take the time to write a personal note.

I have a lot of contacts on LinkedIn, but I don't think any of them ever sent me a personalized note to establish the connection. Everyone uses the standard default note that LinkedIn provides.

It is time to stand out, people. It does not require a lot of effort to draft a quick note inviting someone to connect with you on LinkedIn, but it can truly separate you from the crowd. It leaves a good lasting impression.

#38: Keep confidential information confidential.

There are a lot of things that can trip you up when you first move into a leadership position. There is a lot to learn, and usually a very small window for you to learn it in. One of the things rarely discussed in training for new managers is the impact trust can have.

Trust can have a huge impact in your ability to lead your employees. It can also have a huge impact on how your boss perceives you, which can impact your career progression. In the right circumstances, a breach of trust might even get you fired. I would like to discuss one of those scenarios with you today.

Over the course of my career there have been many occasions where I have known someone was about to be fired or laid off. When someone is about to be let go, there is a planning process that needs to take place to ensure their work is covered by others. As a result, I may know when someone in another department is about to be fired.

If you are in a leadership position long enough, you will likely find yourself in the same position at some point. You are going to know that someone's life is about to change dramatically. It is possible you may have an emotional attachment to that person. Maybe they worked for you at one point, or perhaps you have just become friends over the course of working together for years. There is going to be a strong temptation for you to reach out to them and tip them off that they are about to be let go. You may feel like you are obligated because of your relationship with them, or you just might think it is the right thing to do.

It is not the right thing to do. It does not benefit them. It could get you fired, and it could have significant legal and safety repercussions for your company.

Whether or not you agree with the person's termination is irrelevant. You have to accept you are biased and you likely do not have all of the data you need to make the judgment, anyway. If they are being wrongly terminated that is their issue to tackle, not yours.

How is that person going to react when you tell them? They are being fired, so they have nothing to lose. What's to stop them from storming into their boss's office and letting a few choice words fly on what they think about the boss's opinion? At that point, your friend is still going to be fired, and their boss is surely going to track back the leaked information to you. Whether they can prove it or not may not matter. Perception is enough to kill your career in most cases.

What do you gain by tipping someone off? Their fate doesn't change, but yours might. It does not seem like a very logical thing to do, but I have seen more than one manager do it. Every case I have seen has ended badly for everyone involved.

Take my advice, if you know someone is about to be fired, keep it to yourself.

#39: Focus on employee management.

A lot of experts like to focus on the ways you should set goals for your employees. There are hundreds of websites that will tell you everything you need to know about setting the right goals for your employees. Setting the goals is not where most managers fail. The fail when they do not check in with their employees in regular intervals to ensure they are still on track to accomplish those goals.

Performance goals are designed to help you improve and manage performance. They can only do that if they remain relevant through the year. If they are put in a drawer to collect dust until the end of the year, they are not very likely to drive any kind of performance.

There needs to be adequate communication between you and your employees throughout the year. The first thing you need to do is determine the frequency in which you want to provide feedback to you employees. My personal feeling is that it cannot be less than quarterly, but I think monthly and/or weekly meetings are better options if you have the ability to do it. These meetings do not have to be long, but they have to take place.

There are two things you are trying to accomplish at these meetings.

1. Status Check

Both you and your employee should quickly review each of their goals and look at any relevant metrics to see where they are against them. You could have your employee pull the relevant data ahead of time and present it at the meeting. This makes their goals much more visible to them and also gets them in the habit of monitoring their performance. By conducting the meeting on regular intervals, it also clearly sends the message that these goals are important to you.

2. *Obstacle Removal*

If the employee is not progressing as expected on their goal or they anticipate problems in the near future, this is an excellent time to discuss why and what you can do about it. If you don't have these meeting frequently throughout the year, it is possible that this discussion never takes place, and the goal simply goes unaccomplished. Having the discussion allows you to brainstorm possible solutions to any problems that may come up.

This collective problem solving approach also becomes a great development tool. By showing the thought processes you use to resolve issues, you will help the employee become a better problem solver. There also may be some obstacles they will need your help to resolve. If that is the case, try to resolve those issues as quickly as possible. Dragging your feet on overcoming the obstacle will send a very clear message that the goal is not important.

You can also schedule group status meetings where each member of a team can update the entire team on the progress they have made. Involving an employee's peers can be a strong motivating factor.

This approach also helps educate the entire group on the types of challenges that may occur and how to overcome them. I like using the group approach, but it should not completely replace the one-on-one meeting.

#40 Plan for succession.

Succession planning is a term that I have heard mentioned quite a bit over my career. I have a little confession to make; I am not really sure what the term means. The first time I heard it, I thought it meant I needed to ensure that someone was ready to fill my job in case I left the company. That seemed like an odd way to spend my time. If I prepared someone really well, then maybe I could lay myself off afterwards.

Clearly there has to be more to succession planning than just preparing for my eventual departure from the company. Desperate to find answers,

I turned to the internet. I did not find the answers that I sought. Instead I found some amazing examples of "experts" telling me how important succession planning is, but not offering any tangible recommendations on how to actually go about it.

Disgusted with a lack of answers, I have decided that I will take a shot at explaining exactly what a good manager should be doing to account for a succession plan.

Here is my guide to succession planning in three easy steps.

1. Develop your team.

For each person on my team, I have thought about what skills they need to develop to prepare them for positions of greater responsibility. I have devised a plan on how I can help them to develop those skills.

For example, I think several of my managers need to develop their financial acumen. I have devoted some time each month I can go over the department's P&L with them. It will take a while to get them where they need to be, but we are certainly progressing.

If you have difficulty coming up with areas of development for your team members, try to think about tasks you currently do that you think that they might struggle with. If they are not good public speakers, look for opportunities for them to speak. Help them to develop their presentation and coach them on how to deliver it. If they lack technical expertise, allow them time and resources to develop their expertise.

There are hundreds of skills they may need to develop and thousands of ways to do it. The only trick here is to make sure you are doing something to develop your employees.

2. Develop your team.

This was not a typo. After you have decided what skills your team members need to develop and drafted a plan to do so, then next step should be to ask them what skills they think that they need to develop. I think most of us know what skills we need to develop.

Help your employees to determine a skill or two that they want to work on and draft a plan on how they can develop those skills. Whether you agree with their assessment or not is irrelevant. The key here is to ensure that they are doing something to develop themselves.

3. Set checkpoints.

Most people are capable of executing on the first two points. They will draft beautiful development plans with every intention on executing on them, but then life will get in the way. Things will get busy and the plan will get moved to a drawer never to see the light of day again. We are not going to let that happen.

After you and your employees draft these development plans, you are going to schedule a quick one-on-one meeting to check the progress. These meeting can be monthly and very quick. What did you have planned for the month and did it happen? If it did, then plan out the next month. If it did not, what was the problem, and how can we reschedule what needs to be done? Go ahead and schedule those meetings for the remainder of the year.

In my opinion, you cannot plan for the future. I cannot plan who is going to fill my role if I leave the company. It may be years before I leave, and the person I pick to fill my position may leave a month before me. While you may not be able to plan for the future, you can certainly prepare for it. By actively spending time developing all of my employees, I am preparing them for whatever opportunities may be in the future.

#41: Hire leaders for leadership positions.

I work in a fairly technical field. It takes a several months, if not years, to build up a functional competence. Whenever we have a new management position open, the employees will generally assume the person with the most functional expertise will be the best fit for that position. I think this is a trap a lot of managers fall into as well.

Functional expertise is certainly valuable, but it does not necessarily carry a lot of weight when deciding who to promote into a management position. General Electric is famous for moving their leaders around in the organization. They have a very diverse group of product and services, and their thought process is that a good leader should be able to run any product line, regardless of their experience with that particular product line. Do you think that is true? Can a good leader run any organization?

I do think there is a lot of truth to this thought process. A good leader is a good leader. If they do not have a large amount of technical expertise, I think it is important they have access to people with that expertise. I do feel, however, there is a base level of functional knowledge required for all positions. I don't think I am qualified to be the head of medicine at my local hospital, but I do think you could put me into a variety of other businesses and I would be successful.

I guess my point here is when you are trying to fill leadership positions, make sure you are looking for a leader and not the most technically competent person. The best employee does not always make the best manager.

#42: Use report cards to drive performance.

As a leader, you are expected to provide vision and direction to those you are responsible for leading. It is part of the job description. What happens when you are unable to provide direction? What are you supposed to do when you do not know what direction to go in?

I am sure some folks out there will argue that a leader should never show doubt. They should confidently lead their team in a direction, even if they are unsure. If you are one of those people, feel free to disagree with everything I am about to say.

I don't always have the answers. There are unusual circumstances that sometimes perplex even me. I am not afraid to let people know. I will give you an example. Each week, I send out a report card to all of my direct and indirect reports. The report shows three goals that we have for our department and how we are doing against them. Each result is color coded. It is green if we are hitting the goal, yellow if we are within 10% of hitting the goal, and red if we are missing the mark.

In addition to the report card, I include my own commentary on each goal. If we are in the green, I usually take a moment to express my appreciation in general, but also acknowledge anyone that has made a special effort to keep us in the green.

If we are in the yellow or red I will acknowledge our efforts, but I will point out things we need to do differently if we want to hit the goal. Occasionally, I may run out of ideas on what we can do differently to hit our goals. I am not afraid to ask for help. Each week when I send out the report card I invite any ideas or suggestions on how we might be able to improve our performance. I have received some absolutely wonderful ideas that, quite frankly, I am not sure I would have come up with on my own.

It is important to be confident as a leader. It is a very fine line between confidence and arrogance. When you start thinking you have all of the answers and you arbitrarily dismiss the ideas of those around you, I can promise you your team is not performing at its best. I don't care how smart or experienced you are. You will never have all of the answers.

I learned this lesson the hard way a few years back. My company did a 360 evaluation one year, and one of my direct reports was smart enough to let me know I have a tendency to dismiss other people's ideas. It hit me like a brick. I went through a short denial period, but I slowly realized that she was right. It took a lot of effort for me to change that habit, but it never would have happened if she had not been bold enough to speak up.

#43: Continue to seek self improvement.

Most days I think I am a pretty good manager. I do have a few not so stellar moments. I am not always as patient as I should be with people. I can be a little defensive at times, and I certainly do not praise my folks as often as I should. I have other bad traits that come into play from time to time, but I think most of us do. What about you? Are there moments where you are not the best leader you can be? I suspect if you look really hard, you may find a few.

I am not trying to dwell on the negative, but it is important you realize your bad traits. The main reason you need to be aware of them is so you can make an effort or a plan to overcome them and be a better manager. Another reason you need to be aware of them is your direct reports are aware of your shortcomings as a manager. Not only are they aware of them, but they are likely to adopt your management traits.

One of the things that really makes me strive to be the best manager, leader, and human being I can be is I know there are people following my lead. Whether I want to be their leadership role model or not, I am. Whether they want to admit they are looking at me as a role model or not, they are. I see it in them every day.

I compared the annual reviews I wrote for my direct reports to the annual review my boss completed on me. There are very striking similarities in them, and I take great pride in that as I think all of my direct reports are pretty good managers. It also scares me a little, in a good way. Bad traits get passed on just as easily as good traits. Be very careful of the example you are setting.

I think one of the most important examples you can provide, is one that demonstrates you are constantly seeking self-improvement. I see a lot of managers and leaders at lower levels that are constantly seeking self-improvement. Through training, reading, or formal classes, they are always trying to learn new things. I do not see it nearly as much at the senior levels and that is very troubling. There is no level in the organization you can get to where you can simply stop trying to be better. Senior managers need to seek to improve their skills, if for no other reason than to set a good example.

If you are in a senior leadership position, what example are you setting on self-improvement?

#44: Monitor employee turnover rates.

Employee turnover is something that every manager and leader should keep a very close eye on. Aside from the astronomically high costs of recruiting and onboarding new employees, employee turnover is the single best indicator of employee dissatisfaction.

If you have a large percentage of employees giving their notice, you as a leader need to be concerned. If you have a large percentage of employees quitting without giving notice, you have a crisis that needs to be dealt with immediately.

There can be thousands of reasons for employee turnover, but the first step in reducing turnover is to start talking to your employees. Why are they disgruntled? Talk to as many as you can and listen to their concerns. Just letting them know that someone cares enough to ask why they are unhappy is a step in the right direction to reducing turnover. Once you hear their complaints, resolve the ones you can and take the ones that are beyond your control to your boss. Take their list of issues, but also take your own list of possible solutions.

Here are a couple of other things you can do to reduce turnover.

1. Start with basics.

When new employees start, make sure you are orienting them. Never let a new employee eat lunch alone on their first day with the company. If you can't go to lunch with them, ask one of your other employees to go, and maybe introduce them around. The hard part about starting a new job is you do not know anyone. Help them break the ice.

2. *Change the way you are hiring.*

If you are losing employees consistently in the first ninety days of their employment, something is going wrong in the hiring process. Change it up. Use different interviewers. Post job announcements in different places. Try using a staffing agency. Follow up a little more closely with employees in their first ninety days. Do something that will help to break the cycle of losing people in the first ninety days.

3. *Be realistic with your expectations.*

You have to meet the needs of your clients and do what is best for your company, but be realistic with your overtime expectations. Your employees are entitled to a life outside of work. Give them the opportunity to have one. Forced overtime on a consistent basis is never a good idea.

4. *Stay in the loop.*

Stay in contact with your employees. I like to walk into our break room and just sit down with whoever happens to be in there. Sometimes we talk about their personal lives and sometimes we talk about things that are bothering them at work. The more you talk to your employees, the more likely they are to come to you when they are unhappy. If you manage other managers, make sure they are walking around and engaging with their employees.

Never ignore employee turnover, as it is usually an indication of a much bigger problem.

#45: Put your game face on everyday.

It is Monday morning. This morning I will interact with dozens of people. Most of which will ask me some version of the question, "How are you?" In turn, I will ask many of them the same question. A fairly large percentage of the people I ask that question of, come back with negative responses, such as the following:

"I would be great if it wasn't Monday"

"Okay, I guess"

"Tired, the weekend was not long enough"

If you are a manager, I want you to really put some thought into what your answer is going to be if one of your employees asks how you are. You set the tone for your employees. If you want your workplace to be a happy place that people look forward to coming into, start with the vibe that you are sending out in the morning.

I am absolutely fantastic today. I am healthy, employed, at least I assume so as I have not read my email yet, and I am blessed enough to work with people I care very deeply for. All things considered, I am fantastic and I am ready to shake things up and solve some problems.

Don't be that negative person in the office, especially if you are the manager. Set the tone and be a leader. Your attitude plays a big role in how people perceive you. I don't want to be around negative people. I don't think most people do. Don't be that negative person in the office.

#46: Encourage decision making.

I have heard many a manager complain about some staff member. Some of it is just venting (full disclosure, I may have complained once or twice myself), but many times the manager is genuinely frustrated that their employees seem unwilling to solve any problems that come up. Instead, they come to the manager and expect them to solve the problem.

If this describes your situation, I can assure you this is a learned behavior. If every time I experience a problem, I bring it to my manager and they solve it for me, I will very quickly learn that is the process I should follow. I will be shocked at the end of the year when my manager tells me I lack problem solving skills.

The reality is we do not know if I lack problem solving skills as I have never tried to solve a problem. There is an expression that goes, "If it is not broken, then don't fix it." In this scenario, all of my problems are being solved satisfactorily by my manager, why should I fix that process? It's working beautifully.

As a manager, your primary responsibility is to help develop the talents of the people that report into you. One of the ways you can help them to develop their problem solving skills is to let them take a shot at solving a few problems.

Every one of my direct reports knows what my expectation is. If they come to me with a problem, they need to come to me with some proposed solutions. I want to know they have actually put some thought into the issue before they bring it to me. We did not get to this point overnight; I have worked with all of my direct reports for years. (It pays to have zero turnover.).

I established my expectations fairly early on. When they came to me with an issue, we would talk it out. I would ask them what the possible solutions could be. We would talk about the logic behind our options and decide on the best course of action. Eventually, my role in the conversation becomes less and less until we get to the point they can pretty much go through the process without me.

I can tell you with all sincerity, my managers rarely bring me issues. It is not that we don't have issues, but rather they have developed the ability to handle most things by themselves. When I take a day off, my phone is not blowing up with urgent calls, nor am I getting urgent emails.

The reason I can enjoy a little time off is because every one of my direct reports can diagnose a problem and develop a course of action to overcome it. I may not agree with their decisions every single time, nor is it necessary that I do, but I am always confident they used good logic in reaching their solution.

I strongly encourage you to stop taking on issues from your direct reports. Talk through situations with them and get them to start considering the solutions to a problem before they bring it to you. This may be a big change for you, but you are capable of doing it. You just have to set the expectation.

The flip side is also true. Even if you are a manager, you still report to someone. If you need to let them know about a problem that has come up, also let them know about the possible solutions you have thought through to resolve the problem. I appreciate anyone that takes the time to actually look at the problem before they just come running to me. I think that most managers do.

#47: Act as a shield (sometimes).

I work in a very technical field. It is very easy for one of my employees to make a very innocent mistake that has catastrophic consequences. Then everyone in the company wants to know who made the made mistake. They want to know how I as a manager am going to deal with it. They want to know that justice will be served. It will, but I am going to serve it in my own unique way.

Most of my staff has been with me for a very long time. They take their jobs very seriously and they are diligent about not making mistakes. They are not perfect, and a mistake can sometimes still happen. When it does, there is usually no one that feels worse than the person who made it.

In this scenario, there is really no need for me to do a lot of coaching. They are aware they made the mistake. They already feel more remorse than I would be capable of imparting upon them, and they are extremely clear on the point that they cannot make a habit of making these types of errors. They have already corrected the behavior, and they are completely mortified that everyone in the company knows they made the mistake. From a coaching perspective, there is not really much left for me to coach on. What I can do is offer them a little support.

If they are already punishing themselves for making the mistake, there is no need for me, or anyone else, to pile on as well. Instead, I am going to let them know I have their back and this too shall pass. I am going to be the buffer between them and anyone else in the organization that wants to see their head on a stick. It is the manager's job to take the heat. When those above me ask what I am doing about the situation, I can look them in the eye and respond with:

"I personally met with the employee and I can assure you they are abundantly clear that this type of error will not be tolerated. They fully understand the situation this puts us in, and I am quite confident that it will not happen again."

In reality, I may have met with the employee and reassured them they are still a valuable part of the organization and I don't want them to over-react to this. They already knew this type of error would not be tolerated, so there was no need for me to actually say it.

I am not suggesting that you never coach your employees when they make an error. I am a big advocate of coaching. What I am saying is in those times that everyone else in your organization is condemning one of your employees, that is probably the time to show them a little support. They will remember that and be forever loyal in most cases.

I know that I have done some pretty stupid things over the course of my career, and I can remember vividly each of the bosses that shielded me from the angry mobs and I can also remember the bosses that just joined in with the mob. Which do you want to be remembered as?

#48: As a new manager, try to say something nice.

There are a lot of things that can trip a new manager up when they first take over a new team. The honeymoon phase does not always go exceptionally well. The employees are always going to start off with little or no trust in the manager until that manager earns their trust, and the manager is trying hard to make a good impression for their new boss. This combination of factors can be a recipe for disaster.

As a new manager, your boss is likely to give you an overview of your team, and let you know some of the challenges you are going to face. It is highly unlikely that everything will be perfect with the team you inherit, and there will be a few areas of concern that your boss will want you to focus on. A reasonable person would jump right in and start focusing on those areas of concern and making the changes necessary to alleviate any performance issues.

I am not saying I would not do that, but I might go about it a little differently. I like to take a little bit of time and sit with each person on the team and learn about them and what they do. I am in a purely listening phase at this point. I want them to tell me whatever they want to tell me. I am not going to focus on anything. I am going to let the conversation flow where it may.

After meeting with each employee, I am going to make sure I write down all of my observations in great detail. Hopefully I have a number of positive observations to go along with any concerns I might have.

Later that day, or the next, I am going to thank each employee for their time and call out one of the positive observations that I made. Something like this:

"Hey, Karen, I just wanted to thank you for a taking a few minutes to train the 'new guy'. I must say I was thoroughly impressed with the enthusiasm you attack your job with each day. It was inspiring to me. If you think of anything else you forgot to mention to me, please do not hesitate to stop by or send me an email."

I have now started our relationship off on the right foot. I hate to see new managers come in and immediately attack things they consider to be wrong. It sends a very bad message to the employees and immediately puts them on the defensive.

When you have been on board for a day, it will be tough to win over people that have worked there for years by telling them they are doing things the wrong way. They may very well be doing them the wrong way, but it is worth investing an extra day or two to find a few positive notes to start out on.

The Ken Blanchard Company did a survey of 1,400 executives and they found failing to provide appropriate feedback is the most common mistake that leaders make. Look for opportunities to celebrate success and provide a little positive feedback when you first come into a new management role. It will make your future a lot easier.

#49: Manage your manager.

Even bosses have bosses. How do manage your manager? Before you answer, let me explain the question in greater detail. "Manage your manager" seems to have a very negative connotation. It sounds like I am suggesting you manipulate your boss. That is not at all what I am suggesting.

I do think if the relationship between you and your boss is strained, you need to take ownership and try to fix it. You need to be making a conscious effort to obtain the best possible results for you and your boss. So perhaps a better question would be this: Is the relationship between you and your boss strained? Could it be better?

If you are struggling to maintain a productive and harmonious relationship with your boss, I have a few suggestions.

1. Identify exactly what you believe the issues may be.

Is your boss inconsiderate, do they not provide positive feedback, or do they fail to provide any feedback? What exactly is your issue with them? Are there ways you can work around the issue?

For example, if your boss does not provide enough feedback, you can ask very direct questions, like, "Hey, I finished the productivity report. Did it have everything you needed in it?" It is not ideal, but it will give you a little more feedback.

2. Consider if you are part of the problem.

I have my flaws and you have your flaws. Are you communicating enough? What signals are you sending with your non-verbal communication? Do you get defensive when criticized?

If you have a troubled relationship with your boss, you need to be open to the idea that part of the problem may reside with you. What can you do to improve the situation?

3. Improve communication.

This is by far the most important tip I can give you if you are having issues with your boss. A higher quantity and quality of communication will make your relationships better with just about anyone, including your boss.

If you do not have a regular, preferably weekly, meeting with your boss currently, ask if they would be agreeable to setting one up. If they agree to it, make sure you take the time to prepare for the meeting. Provide updates on where you are in relation to any objective that you have.

Ask your boss if they have any suggestions on anything you should be doing differently. Provide updates on any projects you have been assigned. Go over what your priorities are going to be for the next week, see if they agree.

Make sure you go prepared to the meeting so that you are not wasting your boss's time. If you can successfully get your boss to agree to this meeting, I think it may have a profound impact on your relationship.

4. Make your manager look good.

It is hard to not like and cherish someone that makes you look good on a regular basis. What goals and objectives does your boss have? How can you help them achieve those goals? Do they have a cost cutting goal? What costs can you cut?

Bring them ideas. Help them look good in the eyes of their boss. This is yet another topic you can talk about in your weekly meeting.

5. Decide if it is time to go.

There are too many variables for me to tell you whether you should stick it out and try to forge a better relationship with your boss, or whether you should look for another job. I will say I think most people tend to panic and seek other employment before they have put a sincere effort into improving their relationship with their boss.

If you are miserable and there are no signs it will improve anytime soon, you need to do what you need to do. Either way, make a plan and make it happen.

#50: Learn from your boss.

I have mentioned before that I honestly cannot remember ever having a bad boss. I have heard tales of some absolutely horrible bosses, but I personally have not experienced a horrible boss. If you are stuck with a bad boss and trying desperately to find a new opportunity, I would also encourage you to take a few moments to evaluate your current situation.

How did it come to this? If you are in a situation that is not bearable and you hate coming to work every day, think about the decisions you made that got you here. If your current boss is the one that hired you, what makes you think you next boss will be any better? I know it is a tough job market out there, but you don't want to take the first job offer you get just because it has to be better than where you are.

I am here to tell you that whatever your current situation is, it can get worse. Instead of jumping at the first job offer you get, which is probably what got you into this mess in the first place, perhaps try to be just a wee bit more logical in the selection process.

What questions can you ask interviewers that will increase your likelihood of finding a good boss at your next job? It has been a while since I went on a job interview, but I know I grilled my last interviewer. He was the gentleman that hired me into my current position, and he ended up being my boss for six years. I asked him questions about his education, his accomplishments, how he ended up in his current role, and a variety of questions about his management philosophies.

He would later tell me he felt like I was the one hiring him. I think that is the way you have to be. The interview works both ways. It is a chance for the company to pick the best applicant, but it is also a chance for the applicant to determine if this is a boss that will help to develop and inspire them.

If you just accept any job offer you get based on the money, don't complain when you hate your job and your boss. It is just as much your fault as theirs.

What can I learn from my horrible boss? Most bosses have a few good traits as well as a few bad traits. I have not seen a boss that could not do anything right or one that could not do anything wrong.

There is always something you can learn from your boss. Keep this in mind as you develop your management philosophy. If your boss never communicates with you, what can you learn from that? If that makes you feel unhappy and unappreciated, how will you ensure your employees never feel that way? What are you going to do differently?

I have had bosses that did not have a great grasp on what their employees did all day. I learned very early on that I did not want to be that guy. I know exactly what every person that works for me does. I know it in great detail. That knowledge helps me in a lot of different ways, but it is a habit I picked up because I learned from someone else's bad habit. So back to my original question: What can you learn from your horrible boss?

I hope I have a few new managers or even want to be managers reading this. You are the future. You are the ones that are going to start the management revolution where poor management will not be tolerated. However good or bad your boss is, learn from them.

What is the most important thing you learned from your current or a former boss?

#51: Know that money cannot buy managerial skills.

As a leader, one of my primary responsibilities is motivating others. There are a lot of different theories and perspectives on the best ways to motivate employees. Over the years, I have had a number of people suggest to me that money can be a great motivator. Do pay increases and bonuses have a dramatic impact on performance?

After twenty years of dangling carrots, my answer is maybe. If money does provide a positive motivation for employees, it will be short-term and will ultimately have a negative impact over the long-term. That's right! I am suggesting that pay increases and bonuses will ultimately have a long-term negative impact on your ability to motivate your employees. Think I am crazy? Let me give you a scenario:

I have an entry-level employee that makes $20,000/year and they are a superstar. Going above and beyond every day and really helping my business to retain our clients and attract new ones. The economy is booming and my business is making a lot of money.

At the end of the year, I decide to share the wealth and give them a $2,000 bonus. You can imagine the impact that would have. They would be thrilled and highly motivated. So the next year they work even harder. Only problem is that the economy starts to slow down, and the company barely gets by.

End of the year rolls around, and I am certainly not in a position to be giving bonuses, so I don't. How do you think that employee is feeling after they worked even harder and they did not get anything at all? How would you feel? Do you think they are motivated to work even harder during the next year? I have managed through this scenario, and I have done my best to communicate the reality of our situation at the end of the year.

Some folks get it and are thankful to still be employed and other folks do not and are bitter and angry. Deep down in our hearts, I think most people equate performance with pay. They feel if they work hard they deserve a good raise. Unfortunately, it does not always work like that.

I think that in every company I have ever worked, the commissioned sales people tended to be the highest paid people in the company. Ironically, this is also the position that seems to have the highest turnover rate. Apparently money is not a big enough motivation to get them to stay at one company.

I honestly believe that money is a poor way to motivate employees. I think it is the shortcut for lazy or inexperienced managers. If you truly want to motivate your employees you need to be engaged, communicate constantly, and provide a great work environment. Money matters, but not nearly as much as a lot of folks think.

What do you think? Would you work for a boss that you really disliked for a few extra bucks?

#52: Be approachable.

We have talked at great length about how important communication is in regards to effective leadership. Communication is a key component in effective leadership, in my opinion. There are many facets to communication. How you communicate, the words you use, when you communicate, and how well you listen can all play a role in your ability to communicate. There are other aspects as well, but the one I want to talk about today is approachability. Are you approachable? Are all of your employees and coworkers comfortable approaching you to raise their concerns? How do you know they are?

I don't think I am approachable. That may surprise you, but it is true. I have a very commanding presence. When I walk into the room there is little doubt that I am in charge. That can be intimidating to some. I have great relationships with a large number of my employees, but not every single one of them. I am slowly but surely trying to change that, so every employee finds me approachable. Here is what I am doing:

1. Remove the physical obstacles.

I have an office, and I know for a fact not every employee feels comfortable coming into it. If I am on the phone or I look busy, not many people will muster up the courage to interrupt me.

I try to get out of the office and spend a little time on my production floor every day. It is an opportunity for anyone to grab me and tell me whatever is on their mind.

I find that some people are still a little intimidated by talking in front of all of their peers, so I also try to make it a point to catch some people in the lunch room when they are on break. Sometimes we may talk business; others times we may talk more personal matters. Regardless, it at least gives us an opportunity to talk.

2. Listen.

A skill I have really worked diligently on over the last few years is listening. If you really want to be approachable, practice listening. People are not going to go out of their way to approach you if they believe you are not going to listen to them.

In addition to listening, try throwing a few additional pauses in when you speak. It gives others the chance to chime in.

3. *Make eye contact.*

If you are trying to type a message into your phone when you are walking, very few people are going to approach you, unless you literally run into them. When you are walking around, make eye contact with as many people as you can. It helps send a non-verbal signal to people that you are more than willing to engage in conversation with them.

4. *Be stupid.*

I never cut an employee off when they are explaining something to me. Even if they are explaining a process I completely understand, I still let them go through their explanation.

I am not playing stupid, but rather, I want to hear it from their perspective. It makes the speaker feel valued when you do not cut them off.

5. *Never leave them hanging.*

I have always viewed my employees as customers. I will generally let them talk until they run out of things they want to say. Sometimes I do have other commitments I need to get to, so it is necessary to cut them a little short.

In those cases, I give them a definitive time I will come back and finish the conversation, and I make sure that I do indeed come back.

HOW TO MANAGE PRESENTATIONS BETTER

The thought of giving a presentation strikes fear into the hearts of many managers. Absolutely anyone can deliver an effective presentation. Like any skill, it must be learned and practiced in order to master it. Presentation skills are important, as they can make or break a career, especially at the more senior levels. Take the time to enhance your presentation skills and perhaps use some of the tips on the following pages to help you.

#53: Start your meetings on time.

Are you guilty of starting your meetings late? Is the reason you start late because all of the participants are not there when they should be? I think business people have become conditioned to meetings starting five or ten minutes late, so no real effort is being made to be punctual. Why should I be on time for your meeting, when I know everyone else will not be?

If you are a manager, you have to break this cycle. I have a few tips on how you can, but it only take a commitment from you to make it happen.

Say it out loud: "I will start my meetings on time."

Here are a few more tips to help you actually accomplish this objective.

1. Invite fewer people.

Only invite people that need to be there and are going to help accomplish the objectives of the meeting. The less people, the more likely everyone will be on time.

2. Make it clear when you are going to start.

Let people know in the invitation that you intend to start on time. Give them fair warning.

3. Start on time.

Regardless of who is present, start the meeting on time. You said you were going to start it on time, now fulfill that promise.

4. Make it a short meeting.

A lot of my meetings last about fifteen minutes. You give me a dedicated team, and I can move mountains in fifteen minutes. It seems like the shorter I make the meeting, the more likely everyone is to show up on time. People like short meetings. If you shorten it, they will come.

5. *Create a penalty.*

Make the one that shows up last take the notes for the meeting and send them out to everyone afterwards. I promise you, people will start getting there on time. Let your team know if everyone shows up on time, you will take the notes.

I was having a discussion about this topic today. I don't have many meetings because I don't like meetings. In an average week, I might have ten meetings. If they all start 5-10 minutes late, that is 50-100 minutes I lose in each week. I told you I can move mountains in 15 minutes; imagine what I can do with 100.

People come late to meetings because it is a learned behavior. It's time to start a revolution. Start your meetings on time, and participants will learn to show up on time. Trust me, it works.

#54: Get over presentation anxiety.

If you are reading this, I think it is safe to assume you either have given presentations or you will give them in the future. Everyone gets nervous before they have to present. The best way I know to overcome that anxiety is by practicing your presentation or speech. That's probably not what you wanted to hear, but there is no short cut. Good presentations are the result of preparation and rehearsal. Musicians, actors and politicians rehearse, and so do good presenters.

At a minimum, I would recommend practicing at least three times before actually delivering your presentation. Write out everything you want to say word for word. When you rehearse for the first time, read directly from what you have written, but try to do it with passion. Make sure to inflect your voice at the appropriate points. The second time you go through it, have your notes handy and refer to them when necessary, but try to do as much of it without notes as you can. The third time you rehearse, try to do it with no notes, but also time yourself.

If you are supposed to speak for ten minutes, make sure your presentation is ten minutes long. Unless you truly believe the audience will be clinging to your every word, do not go over your allotted time. Trust me when I say the audience will not appreciate it if your presentation is significantly longer than it is supposed to be. They won't remember what you said, but they will remember it took you way too long to say it.

Practice truly does make perfect when it comes to presenting. You might feel foolish practicing, but you will not feel foolish when you blow your audience away.

#55: Present images, not sentences.

I recently had the misfortune of sitting in on a presentation where the presenter was reading from his slides to the audience. Not only was he reading from his slides with his back to the audience the majority of time, but he had also laid out his presentation in bullet points, that were not bullet points. They were sentences. The material was dry to begin with, but the delivery of presentation made it unbearable to sit through. I surveyed the audience and I could see a lot of misery. Don't be this kind of presenter.

I have read that 85% of all information received by the brain is taken in visually. I am not sure how the researchers got to that exact number, but the point was we tend to remember what we see, not so much what we hear. I certainly believe that to be true in my case. I have a tendency to use images to convey my points. If I am discussing a new idea, I may have an image of a light bulb on the screen instead of bullet points outlining my idea.

While speaking, I will cover anything I would have had in my bullet points, but I won't be reading it from the screen. If there is detailed information I want the audience to see, I provide it to them in the form of a handout. If I am talking about a new program to increase customer happiness, I have a picture of a happy customer on the screen. If I am talking about how we are going to increase sales, I might have an image of a handshake or a contract on the screen while I speak about the details of the program. You get the picture (pun intended).

Images can be a very powerful tool in presentations. They do require you to practice your presentation a little more, because you will not be able to read from the screen if you get stuck. The next time you have to make a presentation, see if you can replace one or two of your bulleted slides with images. Get a little practice with it and see if it helps you to engage your audience a little more. I have had some success with it, but I would be curious to know what works for everyone else.

#56: Don't read from your slides.

I recently sat in on a presentation where the presenter committed what I would consider a presentation atrocity. We were in a large rectangular room, the presenter was at one end, and the audience ran the length of the room. In total the room had about 30 people in it. Not an auditorium, but certainly a large boardroom.

I was fairly close to the presenter and I cringed when I saw his second slide. On his second slide, he had to have had about a dozen bullet points in size 12 font. Maybe I am getting old, but I am not sure I could have read that slide if I were standing a directly in front of the screen.

When I saw the slide, I was certainly concerned about the presenter's ability to keep my interest, but his words absolutely horrified me, "I'm sorry. I know you can't read it, but I will tell you what it says."

I am truly not sure what he said after that, as I started pondering why someone would have a slide that they know the audience would not be able to see or gather any information from. What was the value of that slide? Why would you do that to your audience?

Please do not write complete sentences on your slides. Please do not bullet point your complete sentences. Please do not use size 12 font in a presentation, ever. Size 24 is about as small as you can go, and that has to be in a small room. The bigger the room, the bigger the font, as a rule.

I am slowly evolving away from bullet points all together. I still use them occasionally, but not frequently. I find that images have a much bigger impact and keep the audience engaged. If you use compelling images, and perhaps even a little bit of humor, the audience is on the edge of their seat waiting for the next slide.

To recap, the following are five presentation rules I have learned over the course of my career:

1. *Try not to use bullet points and use images.*

Instead, on your next presentation, replace one slide of bulleted information with an image that conveys your message. Trust me; it works.

2. *Limit each slide to one major point.*

Don't try to cram 12 points on one slide.

3. Never go below size 24 font.

If you can't fit your message on the page, you have too much text. Cut it down.

4. Don't read the text from your slide to your audience—ever.

It gives the appearance you don't know the material.

5. Put yourself in the place of your audience.

What is the major point you want them to get from your presentation? Respect them, respect their time, and grab their attention.

#57: Speak slowly.

I think it is safe to say I have sat in on thousands of presentations at this point in my life. In the majority of those presentations, I would say that the speaker was talking way too fast. The most significant thing you can do today to improve your ability to present is to slow down.

I think presenters generally rush for one of two reasons:

1. They are nervous.

While talking fast will get you out of the spotlight quicker, it tends to leave your audience with a bad impression. If you have to go through the effort of preparing the presentation and dealing with all of the associated anxiety, you at least want the presentation to go well, right?

2. They are excited about the content of their presentation.

I am definitely guilty of this one. If I am presenting on a topic I am passionate about, I tend to speak a little faster. If you want your audience to understand what you are talking about, you need to slow it down.

So what can you do about it? First, being aware of it and making a conscious effort to slow down will help immensely. While you are speaking try to focus on enunciating each word. Practice this on strangers. The next time you are out shopping, speak slowly to the store clerk and ensure you are fully enunciating each word. I practice this a lot, and it does help.

The final trick I would recommend would be to practice your presentation several times. While practicing, ensure that you are speaking slowly. Note a few checkpoints in your presentation. If you have a ten-slide presentation and you know from practicing your presentation you should be at the end of slide two at about the ten minute point, then make a mental note of that. When you deliver the presentation, make sure you are ten minutes in when you get to the end of slide two. If not, adjust accordingly.

I have talked to a few presenters that are afraid they will lose the audience if they talk too slowly. I imagine if you talk slow enough this is possible, but I have not seen any presenters that have to worry about this. The way to keep the audience's attention is to have engaging presentation you have practiced numerous times and to vary the tone of your voice. A monotone presentation will bore your audience regardless of how fast or slow that you speak.

In summary:

1. Try to speak slowly and vary your tone when presenting.
2. With strangers, practice speaking slowly and fully enunciating your words.
3. Ensure you have a few time checkpoints in your presentation so that you know if you are speaking too fast.

#58: Understand that it isn't about you.

Have you ever sat in on a presentation where the presenter has spent a few minutes talking about themselves and their many wonderful accomplishments? I have, and I don't think it is a great way to start a presentation. It is not a good way to lead off a presentation and it is not a good way to lead your life.

Don't spend a lot of time talking about what you have accomplished. Spend your time focusing on how you can help your team accomplish more. If you want to experience true success as a manager, you need to instill a sense of belief in each of your people. They need to be confident they can accomplish their goals. Don't focus on advancing your career; spend your time focusing on how to advance the careers of your team members.

When you spend a lot of time focused on your own accomplishments, it actually helps to alienate your team from you. They start thinking they will never be able to do the things you have done, or you don't notice their accomplishments. When you spend your time caring about your team, they in turn will deliver phenomenal results for you. It literally becomes a labor of love.

This may sound like simple advice, but it is something I personally don't see a lot. In the modern era of downsizing, I think more and more managers are starting to worry about themselves and how they appear to those above them. I understand, and I sympathize, but you will never be a great manager if you are your number one priority.

What can you do today to help advance one of your team members? Can you train them on a new skill? Can you help them network a little in your organization? Can you provide them with a new opportunity to shine? Maybe you can send them a little note of praise to help build their confidence. There are a million things you could do, but what are you going to do?

#59 Be careful when using humor in your presentations.

Humor can be a welcome addition to most presentations, but it is never a requirement. I am not the kind of guy that will open with a joke. In fact I have never told a joke in a presentation. I will tell humorous stories if they naturally fit into whatever my presentation topic is. I like to use humor in my presentations because it helps to engage the audience and keep them attentive. It also helps to break down barriers. It is hard to hate someone that makes you laugh.

Is humor an absolutely critical element to delivering an effective speech or presentation? Absolutely not. Many a great speech has been delivered with no humor at all. That does not mean you should not use humor either. If you have a humorous story that is relevant to your topic, you may want to consider using humor, but there are a few other things to consider as well.

1. Your humorous story needs to be original.

If you do not have a humorous story that fits nicely with your topic, don't borrow one. Tell your own stories, because you will naturally be able to deliver them with more passion, which will make for a better presentation all around. You also lose all credibility if someone has heard the story before.

2. *You and your story should be funny.*

You should have a good idea of whether or not you can tell a funny story. If you don't know, you probably cannot do it. Even if you are confident you are funny, your story may not be funny to other people. It's best to try it out on friends or loved ones first. If you get good feedback, consider working it into your speech.

3. *Humor should always be appropriate.*

Know your audience. If there is any doubt in your mind whatsoever about whether your story is appropriate, then leave it out.

4. *You can be self-deprecating, but don't embarrass others.*

Self-deprecating humor can be very effective. It helps to build a bond with the audience. No one wants to hear a self-proclaimed expert speak, but a guy that is willing to laugh at himself can't be all bad. I never tell stories that will embarrass someone else. It is just not professional, and you never know how that other person will react.

Humor is a good presentation tool, but like any tool it takes a lot of practice to get good at it. Get practice in social settings and slowly work your stories into your presentations when it is appropriate. Never force humor into a presentation.

#60: Prepare for your first presentation.

I was terrified the first time I had to speak professionally in front of a group of people. For me, that occasion happened in the military. I was not prepared for the moment at all. No one had offered me any advice or tips on public speaking.

For a first time speaker, I don't think I did too badly. What I lacked in skill I made up for in confidence. Over the course of my career I believe I have become a much better speaker. That has not happened by coincidence. I put a lot of effort into it. When I came out of the military and transitioned into corporate life, I joined Toastmasters.

I do not want to assume that everyone has heard of Toastmasters. It is a non-profit educational organization that teaches public speaking skills. They accomplish this mission by having thousands of Toastmasters clubs throughout the world. If you live anywhere in the vicinity of a metropolitan area, I can assure you there is a Toastmasters club near you. Each of the clubs meets a couple times a month.

At the meetings, there are several people that will deliver prepared speeches, they will receive feedback on what went well during the speech, and they will also get recommendations on things they may want to improve upon. The clubs are great networking events, as they are made up of people that are generally already executives or they aspire to be. Either way, they are good people to know. Toastmasters is a fantastic organization and I cannot recommend them enough.

If you seriously want to become a better speaker, I highly recommend checking their website to find a club close to you. Sit in on a meeting; it may change your life.

Back to my story...

I was thinking about that first time I had to speak the other day, and I thought about how nice it would have been for someone to have given me a few pointers before that presentation. It did not happen for me, but I am going to offer a few presentation tips for beginners. If you have never given a presentation before, here are a few tips to keep in mind:

1. PowerPoint is there to assist you, not the other way around.

You are the presenter. You should have a message. You should be dynamic and engaging. PowerPoint is there to support your message with images or other relevant information when appropriate. Every word you are going to speak should not be on your slides. Use PowerPoint to enhance your messages, not to deliver it. If someone gets a hold of your slide deck and it makes perfect sense to them without having heard you speak, you have too much information on your slides.

2. Avoid bullet points when possible and use images instead.

See previous point.

3. Practice. Then, practice again. Then, practice again.

If I am giving a formal speech, I will go through it a minimum of three times. Once reading from my notes, once trying to wing it but using the notes for support, and finally, without notes all together. Your audience does not want to hear you read. Take the time and prepare. You presentation does not have to be perfect. You may forget a detail here or there and that is okay. I would rather hear a dynamic speaker miss a point, as opposed to one that is reading verbatim from their notes. Look your audience in the eyes and talk to them, don't read to them.

4. *Every presentation is about the audience.*

Put yourself in the shoes of your audience. Why should they care what you are saying? What is in it for them? Even if you find your topic interesting, your audience may not. What can you do to make it interesting for them? What is it you want them to take away from your presentation? Is your message clear and relevant to your audience?

5. *Timing is important.*

If you have been provided a twenty minute time slot to deliver your presentation, make sure it is no more than twenty minutes long. Do not assume what you are talking about is so important that everyone will not mind if you go over your allotted time. They will.

#61: Plan and practice for a great presentation.

One of the things I have noticed working with new managers is they do not like to plan their presentations out. If they have to deliver a presentation, they open PowerPoint and start making slides. When they feel like they covered the topic, they stop making slides. Some of them will practice it before they go up, and others just present it without ever having gone through it. A lot of them can deliver a perfectly satisfactory presentation. It will not knock your socks off, but it will get the job done. If satisfactory is all you are going for perhaps you can adopt this style. If you are looking to leave a positive impression on people, I would suggest focusing a little more effort on planning and practice.

Planning

When you learn you need to deliver a presentation, the first thing you should do is not open PowerPoint, but rather put a little thought into what you are trying to accomplish. Why are presenting? What is the message that you are trying to convey? What do you want people to walk away with and remember? A lot of times when I ask presenters these questions they either have vague answers or no answers at all. A lot of times managers will tell me their goal is to impress the audience. What does that mean? I think the goals needs to be a little more specific than that.

When you are going to speak, consider why you have been asked to speak. What message are you trying to convey? Most importantly, why should anyone in the audience care what you have to say? How can you help them?

Once you have identified what is in it for the audience and what you want them to walk away with, the presentation design gets much easier. After I have figured those things out, I like to start drafting my presentation, but I generally will do this on paper. I just sketch out how I plan to open, what my major points will be, what support I will use for each of those points, and how I will close.

I want to make sure I open with something that will grab the audience's attention immediately and will also let them know what they are going to get from my presentation. I usually try to open with a quick story relevant to the topic. If I am talking about management, I might tell a quick story about a poor management decision I made and how I hope the audience can learn from my mistake.

Everyone loves a good story, and chances are some of the audience members have made the same mistake. What I never do is talk about my qualifications or experience. Introduce yourself, but don't spend ten minutes talking about your qualifications. If you tell a good story and give them something to walk away with that will help them, they probably won't care what your qualifications were. They will just be happy they got to hear you speak.

Once I have the presentation sketched out and I am happy with it, I open PowerPoint and start designing slides. Slide design is not my topic today, so I will keep it brief by saying use images often and do not write out full sentences on your slides. One other thing, don't cram ten points onto one slide that no one can read. Use ten slides that everyone can see clearly instead.

Practice

This is the other half of the equation and it is also something new managers tend not to do. I have had managers give me a lot reasons why they don't practice. I have yet to hear a good one. I have given hundreds of presentations, and no one will convince me that practice does not help.

Here are a few quick tips on how to get the most out of your practice sessions.

1. Get as close to the speech setting as you can.

This means using a projector and standing up while you are talking. If you are using any type of props or visual aids, include them in your practice sessions. Practice in the room you will be using if possible.

2. Time yourself.

If you are supposed to be speaking for ten minutes and you realize you have 100 minutes of material, something needs to give. Either shorten your presentation or work with the meeting organizer to get a bigger time slot. No one will complain if you sit down a minute or two early, but they tune you out if you start running over.

3. Listen closely to yourself or have a friend listen to you.

Does what you are saying make sense? Does it have a good flow? Make adjustments where necessary.

4. Do it more than once.

I practice a minimum of three times before any presentation. Practice does make perfect.

HOW TO MANAGE COMMUNICATIONS BETTER

Every manager needs to communicate effectively. Communication is the basis of all our relationships. In order to perform the basic functions of management, you have to be able to effectively communicate your plans, ideas, and goals. Presenting your ideas to those above and below you in the organization can be a crucial component to your success. I have made a number of mistakes as a communicator over the course of my career, and I have also learned a thing or two about communicating along the journey.

#62: Write attention-getting emails.

Ever get the feeling people are not reading your emails? As someone that gets a very large number of emails each day, let me give you a few insights into how to get your email read.

1. *The subject matters.*

Make sure the reader can clearly understand the topic of the email from the subject line. Don't get clever here, instead be clear and concise. I tend to skip over emails that don't get my attention in the subject line. Sometimes I come back to them; sometimes I don't.

2. *Think before you write.*

If the email is important or going to someone you would like to impress, take a few minutes and think about what you are going to say. Organize your thoughts before you write. For really important emails, I will go as far as to outline what I am going to say. That way I ensure that my points are in a logical order and not a random scattering of thoughts.

3. *Be brief.*

Make your point and provide enough support information to back it up, but don't provide the history of the world. If I get a five page email, there is very little chance I am going to read it word for word. I am scanning it looking for major points instead. Cut the fluff out. The shorter it is, the more likely I am to read it verbatim.

4. *Stay positive.*

State facts in your emails, but try not to draw conclusions. Let the reader draw their own conclusions. Don't say anything in email you would not say to the person face to face. You can direct, but be nice. That's just good advice for life.

5. Don't write angry.

Nothing positive will ever come from sending a harshly worded email. If you are angry, the best advice I can offer you is not to send any emails. True communication cannot take place when you are angry.

#63: Don't kill the messenger.

I work with a lot of people. Some of them irritate the heck out of me. We may have a long history, and somewhere along the line I have labeled them as less than helpful to the organization. Labeling them is probably not good practice, but I can't help it. I am sure there is a personal development goal in there somewhere. At any rate, I have to make a dedicated effort to ensure I am treating them fairly and assisting them when they do have legitimate issues. That is harder than it sounds. When certain names pop into my inbox, I automatically cringe.

The lesson I have learned about this over the years is I have to make a dedicated effort to make sure I am separating the message from the messenger. Even the worst employee on their worst day, can ask a legitimate question that certainly deserves a well thought out answer.

There are going to be people cross your path who you will not like. The reasons why are irrelevant, at least for the purposes of this book, but we still have an obligation to handle communication with them professionally and answer their inquiries, assuming they are relevant and reasonable.

I have found the best way for me to accomplish this is to delay my response slightly. If I respond immediately upon receiving their inquiry, I am far more likely to come across as defensive, dismissive or patronizing. By delaying just a few minutes and rereading the email a second or third time, I am usually able to craft a much more professional reply that actually answers their question.

#64: Communicate effectively.

Do you ever get the feeling that your employees are not listening to you? As a manager you may get that impression every now and then. It most likely stems from the fact they are not listening to you. I have a few quick tips to increase the likelihood that your team may actually listen to your next message:

1. Mix your mediums.

There are times I may change a policy or procedure, and I need to ensure everyone is aware of the change. I may send an email out to my entire team, or I may hold a departmental meeting to announce the change. Sometimes I put notices in the employee lounge and other times I ask my managers to announce the changes in team meetings with their teams. I like to change up the way that I communicate with my employees frequently; I think it helps to keep their attention.

Have you ever had a manager that communicated an important message in a memorable way?

2. Repetition is crucial.

If the message I need to get across is really important, I will ensure that the message goes out more than once. The more important it is, the more likely I am to put the message out multiple times.

There have been thousands of studies that support the fact people will comprehend information more effectively if it is presented multiple times. If you really want to get crazy, send your message out multiple times using different forms of communication. If you are unclear about what I am talking about, please reread point #1.

3. Try not to be negative.

People tend to tune out negative messages. I know I do. See if you can send out a positive message from time to time. There are absolutely times I have to send out negative information, but if you are mingling it with a few positive announcements I think you will find you get a much better reception.

#65: Learn the three things not to say in your next interview.

Most of us have been on both ends of the interview process. To be honest, I am probably not as involved in the new hire process as I once was. My direct reports have not turned over in years, and they handle most of their own interviews. That does not mean I do not have a few suggestions for interviewees. I have interviewed many outstanding applicants over the course of my career, but I have also had a few interviews that did not go well.

Here are a couple of things applicants have said to me that caused me to question whether they would be a good fit in my organization.

To put it in simpler terms, the following are some things you should not say during an interview:

1. *"Do you mind if I get that?"*

On more than one occasion, I have been in the middle of an interview and the applicant's cell phone goes off. Most applicants are absolutely horrified when this happens and they do whatever they can to silence it. You should turn you cell phone off before you go into an interview. However, if you forget and it does ring, but you immediately silence it, I am probably not going to hold that against you.

I did have one applicant that dug her cell phone out of her purse, looked at it, and then asked me if I minded if she took the call. I told her I did not mind as it appeared we were done. (We were five minutes into the interview.) She proceeded to take the call, which from what I could tell certainly did not seem to be any sort of emergency situation.

Maybe I am old school, but I think it takes a lot of audacity to take a phone call during an employment interview. Most interviews take between thirty and sixty minutes. I think most of us can put our life on hold for that time and turn our phones off. If you can't, you're probably not going to perform well in the job, even if you can get past the interview.

2. *"I can start immediately."*

I have to clarify this one. If you are currently not working, this is a completely appropriate and desirable thing to say. If you are currently employed, this is one of the worst things you can say. Many applicants sense the employer needs to get the position filled immediately, so instead of letting the job go to another applicant that can start immediately, they blurt out that they too can start immediately. This is not what I want to hear as an interviewer.

If you are currently employed and you are willing to leave that job with no notice, I have to assume you are going to do the same thing to me. No matter how pressured you may feel, don't ever quit a job with no notice.

I cannot easily count the number of employees that have left my company because they were angry about something at the moment, only to discover several months or years later that they indeed had a pretty good working environment. To date, I have never hired anyone back that left without giving notice.

Don't burn bridges. Feelings change over time, but you cannot always go back and repair the damage.

3. *"I have no questions."*

I certainly try to sell applicants on the company. I want them to want to work here, but time is limited, so I can't go into great detail. If, at the end of the interview, there is nothing you are interested enough in to ask a question about, I am likely not going to be very interested in you.

I like to believe all of my employees work here because this is where they want to work. I don't want to bring people in that are just here to collect a paycheck, I want new hires to want to work here as well.

Look up information about the company where you are interviewing, and think of a few questions before you go into the interview.

#66: Make time to answer quick questions.

As a manager, your employees are testing you every day. They may not even realize they are testing you, but they are. They pass judgment on each interaction you have, or should have had, with them. Sometimes those judgments are good and sometimes they are not so good. Sometimes they are fair and sometimes not so fair.

I covered previously I felt being approachable is extremely important for anyone in a leadership position. You want people to feel comfortable approaching you with ideas, suggestions, or even complaints. It is far better they communicate their thoughts to you than to keep all of their ideas and frustrations bottled up. One of the easiest ways to lose your approachability and have some rather harsh judgments cast upon you is to fail to fully and properly answer a question one of your employees brings to you.

There are times I am very busy and I am getting ready to hustle off to an important meeting. Inevitably that is when one of my employees will grab me and ask me a question about why we have a certain policy or procedure. Even though I am pressed for time, the absolute worst thing I can do at this point is to tell them "that is just the way it is" or "that is just what the policy has always been." Any responses along these lines will kill your approachability. The employee had the courage to initiate contact with the big boss and ask about a policy that does not make sense to them because they have thought of a few better ways that something could be done.

This is exactly the behavior we want from our employees. At this moment we should put them up on a pedestal and praise them in order to encourage other employees to come forward, but instead many managers will brush the question off and provide the shortest answer possible in order to move on with their day. If you do that, then you are sending two very clear messages:

1. *My time is more important than the time of my employees.*

This is the message you will send and I hope you don't start believing this. As a manager, your employees will make or break you. There is no one whose time should be more valuable in your eyes.

2. *Your question is not important.*

Assuming your employees are reasonably competent, they have far more potential to develop better processes than you. They are closer to the actual work. Fail to answer their questions on a regular basis, and they will stop bringing them to you. I would hate to think one of my employees is sitting on a million dollar idea, but is too afraid or apathetic to bring it forward.

Try not to be too busy to answer questions from your employees. If you absolutely do not have the time to give them a proper answer to their questions, thank them for asking the question and let them know you will be back after your next meeting to give them a proper answer. Most importantly, remember to go back.

Getting your employees to come forward with questions and suggestions should be the goal of every manager. What are you doing to ensure that your employees are coming forward with their questions?

#67: Learn to receive feedback well.

I give more feedback than I get. I thoroughly enjoy providing feedback to my employees, but I struggle with receiving feedback. Even it is positive feedback, it usually makes me uncomfortable and that fact probably makes it uncomfortable for the person providing the feedback. This is something that I will be trying to improve upon throughout the next year. I have put a little thought into what needs to be done to improve, and here are some of the items I will be working on:

1. Not Being Defensive

In a previous tip I tried to explain the difference between taking things personally and being defensive. In my mind these are two very different things. Taking things personally means I care. That's a good thing. As managers we want our people to care. Being defensive refers to a situation where I feel like I am being personally attacked, so I feel the need to defend my actions.

Many times this feeling can stem from a simple question, or the simple question could be a veiled attack. Either way, becoming defensive will rarely help the situation. I think the best way to diffuse this is let the other person know you hear them; you understand they are upset and you want to help.

Truly try to listen to them and see if there is a way you can address their concern. Listen to the actual problem and see if you can brainstorm a solution to the problem. Don't focus on right and wrong, rarely is there an absolute right or wrong, focus on problems and solutions instead.

2. Seeking Specific Examples

This is probably the most important thing on this list. I cannot easily count how many times someone has told me a client is unhappy and we need to improve our level of service. What does that mean? My company offers over 100 different services, I need to know which service they are unhappy with. Maybe they are unhappy with our customer service. Maybe they are unhappy with our pricing, or perhaps we messed up their invoice.

In order to fix any problem, you need to gather as many specifics as you can. You do not want to spin your wheels fixing things that are not broken. Even if someone is giving you positive feedback, you want to make sure you understand exactly what they are pleased about. In order to continue doing the good work that I am doing, I need to understand what exactly I am doing so well. Ask clarifying questions.

3. Responding to Content, Not Tone

Sometimes a raving lunatic may raise a good point. Try to calm them and get the content of their concern. Ignore the tone and focus on the message. This is far easier said than done, but it is something we all need to master. This is just self-control.

Don't let yourself get sucked into a confrontation. Learn to recognize it, and make a conscious effort to keep your cool while trying to define the actual issue.

#68: Develop your charisma.

Charisma is like good leadership, it is hard to describe but I know it when I see it. When I think of charismatic people, I think of the people that are able to make everyone they encounter feel special. Is charisma a natural born gift that some have and others never will? I don't think so. I think there is hope for anyone that wants to be a little more charismatic.

There is good reason to want to develop your charisma. Charismatic people are able to positively influence others. Therefore charismatic people can be great salespeople, excellent negotiators, and outstanding leaders.

This was actually one of the first topics I considered writing about when I started my blog. I held off because I wanted to take a little time to observe people I believe demonstrate good charismatic skills. My observations are complete and I now feel like I am in a position to recommend a few things each one of us can do to improve our charisma. The following list is by no means complete, but I think it gives us a few things to focus on for the time being.

The following are four things you can focus on today so you can strengthen your charisma:

1. Eye Contact

I am of the belief that the ability to maintain eye contact with the people you encounter is essential for your success in life. It is also essential if you would like to develop your charisma. When you walk into a meeting room, try to make eye contact with as many people as you can. Don't look down at the floor, up at the projection screen, or off into space. Look the people in the room straight in the eye. Hold it for second then move onto the next person. I don't care who is in the room. Be anyone's equal.

When you are speaking with someone, whether in a large meeting or one-on-one, try to maintain eye contact. Don't stare, but maintain the contact as they speak and glance away at a break in the conversation.

Practice this with your family and friends this weekend. It is easier than you think and it is essential for building a connection with someone.

2. Listening

It may seem obvious that you have to listen to people, but very few people have mastered this skill. To really listen, first you have to stop talking. This alone presents a challenge for many people I know.

Assuming you can silence yourself; the next step is focus on what the person is saying. Empathize with them. Put yourself in their shoes. How would you feel in their situation? Consider how you would feel, but do not start considering what you are going to say next.

I think the reason most of us are not very good listeners is because we only listen long enough to determine what we are going to say next. We are not listening; we are waiting for our turn to talk. I will instantly feel a connection with anyone I think is actually listening to me.

Again, try practicing this on your family and friends first. Truly listen to them. You will be amazed at the impact it has on your connection with them.

3. Pausing

If you are listening to someone you will need to take a second to think before you speak. This is okay. It may feel a little unnatural to you, but you will get used to it. When someone takes a second before they begin to speak, it conveys that they are actually listening and they have given great thought to what they are about to say.

I have noticed the people I have deemed "charismatic" almost always pause a second or two before they speak. It is a good habit to get into, even if you are not concerned about developing your charisma.

Thinking before you speak will help you in just about every aspect of your life. I have worked with many overbearing people that tend to cut others off, or begin speaking the split-second that there is a break in the conversation. It is clear they are not listening to anyone and they are not interested in any opinion but their own. It is very hard to feel a connection with these types of people.

4. *Saying My Name*

Charismatic people will almost always remember your name and use it in conversation with you repeatedly. There is no doubt in my mind this practice helps you to establish a connection with someone.

Likewise, I think it is impossible to feel a connection with the guy you met five times that still can't remember your name. He may be a smart guy, but you can't help but discount everything he says when he calls you by the wrong name.

Practice this. Practice it with everyone you meet. I promise you it will pay off for you.

Here is your homework: Today, I want you to practice maintaining eye contact, listening, and pausing before you speak with your family and friends. It may be a little awkward at first, but stick with it, as I think you will find these worthwhile skills to master.

#69: Don't compare salaries.

How much do you make? It is a rhetorical question, as I truly have no desire to know. Knowing someone else's salary will only cause you pain and heartache. I try to never speculate about salaries or engage in any gossip about the compensation levels of my peers or those higher than me in the organization.

Many years ago, my boss needed some data on a few of my newer employees. He had his administrative assistant send me a spreadsheet with a lot of personal data on it and a few blanks I was to fill in. To my surprise, not only did the spreadsheet contain the salary data for my employees, but it also contained the salary data for every employee the company had hired that year. It included people at every level of the organization.

My first instinct was to close it immediately, but that is not what I did. I read it all the way through. I filled in the information I was supposed to and sent it back. I was smart enough to delete the email and the spreadsheet from my computer, but the numbers stuck in my head. I couldn't help but do comparison between my salary level and the salary levels of those that had been hired in at my level.

When we learn what someone else makes, our instinct is to do a comparison with what we perceive our value to be compared to theirs. This is never a good idea. I do not believe anyone is capable of objectively evaluating their value to the organization. We tend to unfairly weigh the things we do and the value we have. It is human nature. Not only do you unfairly weigh the things you do, but you can never honestly know all the things that someone else does.

My advice to you is to never do those comparisons. I have seen employees that were completely happy in their jobs absolutely lose their minds once they learned what someone else makes in the company. I have had good people quit with no notice and screw up an otherwise stellar career because they felt the compensation system was completely unfair once they learned someone else's salary.

Don't compare your salary to anyone else. No good will come of it. Spend your time contemplating whether you like your job. I am not a big fan of people that like to tell us we should all do what we love and that if you don't love your job, you should quit. If everyone did the world would devolve into anarchy within days.

You should find a job that allows you to provide for you and your family. If you hate that job, stick with it until you find a job you like better that still provides the compensation necessary to put food on the table.

I feel like I am paid a reasonable rate for what I do. I sincerely like my job and I thoroughly enjoy the people I work with. I don't care what anyone else is paid, and most days I am pretty happy.

I don't like to spend a lot of time focused on what I cannot control. I can't control what those above me make. I can control whether I take time to appreciate that I am employed, I have food on my table, and I have pretty good benefits. If I spend my time on that, I find I am a much happier person.

If you want to be happier, stop worrying about what everyone else makes. Appreciate what you have and work on making yourself indispensable. If you do, I promise good things will happen.

#70: Understand that your message is made up of more than words.

It never ceases to amaze me that whenever people are involved in a communication breakdown, they naturally assume the breakdown is the fault of the other person. If one of my direct reports fails to carry out instructions I gave them, I will naturally assume the breakdown in communication occurred with them. That is always my first instinct, but as a semi-enlightened human being, I can usually think about it for a minute and realize the issue may be partially or entirely with me.

There are a lot of things that can impact how effectively you communicate. The words you choose, the moods of the individual's involved, and even body language.

On my recommended reading list, there is book titled *Leadership and Self Deception*. I read the book several years ago. I then developed several training classes based on the concepts in the book and I have successfully delivered those training classes numerous times. I have given the book as a gift over a dozen times as well. The reason that I mention all of this is because the book does an outstanding job of explaining how our behaviors greatly influence the message others receive from us. Maybe even more so than the words we speak. Shaking your head back and forth, constantly looking at your watch, or sitting with your arms crossed can have a profound impact on how your words are interpreted.

Do you think your communication style changes when you are speaking with someone you do not like? I have really been trying to observe my own behavior when I am speaking with people I like, and comparing it to my behavior when speaking with people I may not be as fond of. One thing I have noticed is as the conversation is beginning, I tend to stop and face people that I like. For those I may not be as fond of, I tend to stop and just turn my head when speaking with them. I guess deep down I am trying to send a subtle message that this conversation is not going to last long.

I have also noticed my vocabulary changes slightly depending on who I am speaking with. I am an educated and semi-intelligent person, so I know a few big words. I find those big words tend to get tossed around a lot more when I am conversing with individuals I may not care for.

If I had the time and desire, I am sure I could find dozens of differences in the ways I communicate, but my informal study has provided me more than enough data to conclude I do behave differently depending on how I feel about the person I am speaking with.

What about you? Do you think you communicate differently when you are speaking with someone you may not like? Do you think the people you are communicating with are able to pick up on your non-verbal cues? What impact do you think that has on your ability to communicate with them? Should we be concerned about this, and if so, what can we do to minimize the impact?

#71: Don't make jokes to fill awkward silences.

I mentioned in a previous post that I am an early bird. I like to get into the office and knock a few things out before the crowd comes in. On the flip side, I like to leave on time. I have many interests outside of work, so I usually have things I am looking to get done in the evenings. The other day I was leaving at a little after 5:00 p.m. (keep in mind that I come in at 7:00 a.m.), and a manager from another department said, "Hey, I wish I could work your schedule."

I know this is harmless banter designed to eliminate that awkward silence as we pass each other, but it irritates me greatly because there are so many flaws in their logic.

There are a number of things I would like to say back:

1. "You can work my schedule, but you would have to come in two hours earlier, which I sincerely doubt you are capable of."
2. "It is amazing how much you can get done when you actually work all day. You should try it."
3. "Doesn't it bother you that I leave before you each day and I still consistently outperform you?"

I refrain from saying any of those things because the damage I would do is not worth the joy that I would feel (but it would feel good).

Your homework assignment for today is to ensure you are not criticizing anyone for the time they leave, the time they come in, or the fact they take a lunch, even jokingly. Any one of these things taken out of context is not enough for you to draw any kind of conclusion about the person's work ethic or their ability to get things done. Making jokes about any of these things only serves to irritate people. The jokes are not funny.

#72: If you are going to quit, do it correctly.

Unfortunately, I think most of us are going to have to work for several different employers over the course of our career. The days of working for one employer for twenty plus years seem to be behind us. I hope I am wrong on that, but if all the people I know are any indication, I think you should be educated on exactly how to go about quitting your job.

1. Tell your boss first.

Don't tell your friends in the company first. No matter how much you trust them, people will talk. You do not want your boss to hear it from someone else.

2. Put it in writing.

This should be the shortest letter you have written. Try not to say much other than that you are leaving, when your last day will be, and you are grateful for the experience. This is not the time to write a manifesto on why you hate your boss or the company. After you quit, any criticisms you may have of your boss just sound like sour grapes. Your complaints would have been much more meaningful when you were an employee. If you kept your mouth shut for years and never complained about anything, keep your mouth shut for two more weeks. It is not worth venting. You are not going to bring about change at this point, and anything you put in writing may come back to haunt you later. Just let it go.

3. Give at least two weeks' notice.

This is a standard practice and if you fail to provide the appropriate notice, many companies will mark you as ineligible for rehire. I cannot easily count the number of employees that have left with no notice, only to call back at a later point to see if they can get their job back. There are very few absolutes in my life, but I never hired someone back that failed to give the appropriate notice.

4. Help to transition your work.

Give your boss a detailed plan of the things you do, so they may draft a suitable plan for replacing you. Also help to train anyone your boss identifies in your duties.

5. Actually work your last two weeks.

I have asked many an employee to leave before their two weeks were up. If you are only going to serve to be a distraction during your last two weeks, I would rather you just leave.

Most people are only going to find a new job when they are looking for one. They are looking for one because they are unhappy in their current position for any one of a million reasons. When they find a new job, they are thrilled. They feel liberated, as if they have been paroled from prison. That feeling of elation causes them to make stupid decisions. They violate one or more of the five rules I posted above because they are sure that their future is bright, and they will never need their old employer again. This is a fool's logic. How can you possibly be sure your new job is better than your old job until you actually start working it? You can't.

When the time comes to leave your job, do it professionally. Follow these rules and maintain all of your contacts at your previous employer. One thing I know is it is a small world and your reputation is worth protecting. Treat others as you would expect to be treated, and that includes when you quit.

#73: Value appreciation—the gift that keeps on giving.

I love Fridays. There is a magic in the air and most folks are just a little bit happier. Friday is a great day to let an employee or a coworker know just how much you appreciate them. You have the power to make someone's day, and since it is Friday, that positive feeling will likely stick with them through the weekend. What could be better? So what is stopping you from making it happen?

1. Send a thank-you email.

Thank a co-worker for something they helped you with this week. Include their boss if you want.

2. Write a thank you card.

Take the time to write a thank you note for one of your employees that has really had a good week. Be specific about why you appreciate them and the value they add to your organization.

3. Give a small gift card to your housekeeping personnel.

My office is always cleaned, trash always emptied, and I never see our housekeeper. She is like a housekeeping ninja. It is one of those jobs no one appreciates unless it is not done well. I love the housekeeper we have, but I bet she does not know how much I appreciate her. Time to change that.

4. Give a book to someone as a thank you.

I love when people recommend books to me. I love it even more when they just hand me a book. You can thank them and help to develop them at the same time.

5. Ask someone to lunch.

Ask someone today who you do not normally go to lunch with. Break out of your rut. Talk to new people. Forge new relationships.

6. Connect with your connections.

Go into your LinkedIn account and reach out to someone who you have not spoken with in over a year. Just ask them how they are doing. Actually connect with your connections.

Take today as an opportunity to make a little gesture that will make someone else feel appreciated. It is these little things that keep employee turnover low and productivity high.

#74: Follow these five quick tips for being successful.

Most people are not incredibly successful. Whatever your definition of successful is, if you believe most people do not meet the definition it is safe to assume the successful people are in the minority. If that is true, logically one should focus on doing things most people do not do if you want to be successful. To that end, here is a list of things I believe most people do not do that can help you to be more successful, using whatever definition of successful you have:

1. Get up earlier.

Most people do not like to get up early. I get at 5:00 a.m. or a little before each day and write. It is completely quiet in my house, and I find I tend to be a little more creative first thing in the morning.

2. Exercise.

I am far from an Olympic athlete, but I do work out consistently. I talk to so many people that tell me they would like to work out, but... Exercising puts me in a better mood, better shape, and better health. Make time for exercising.

3. Write your goals down.

You are exponentially more likely to accomplish your goals if you write them down. Create professional goals, financial goals, relationship goals and goals around whatever else is important to you. Define what success will look like.

4. Step out of your comfort zone.

You have to break out of your comfort zone and take risks. Try a new dish, take a class, but get out there and mix it up. Spending another night watching television is not going to get you closer to achieving your goals.

5. Starting right now, stop putting things off.

If you are committed to exercising, exercise today. If you are committed to writing your goals down, do it today. Stop putting off success.

#75: Handle disagreements professionally.

I was never on the debate team in high school. I probably should have been, because I have always been a fierce debater. Especially in my younger days, I knew everything and I was on a mission to prove to the world I was right, on every topic.

As I have gotten older and discovered I know next to nothing, I find I like to debate things far less. Part of the reason is when you have a disagreement with someone, sometimes you lose even though you may convince them you were right.

Depending on how vehemently you disagree, and how you present your case, you may make your point, but the other person may lose all respect for you in the process.

Having irritated more than my share of people in life, I thought I would share the following rules I have developed for handling disagreements:

1. *Don't have them.*

This is by far the best tip I can give you. Some battles are not worth fighting. If someone says something you know is incorrect and it is not going to have any bearing on your company or your life, let it go. It is generally not worth proving the other person wrong. It does not make you look smarter, it makes you look arrogant.

No one likes a know it all. Let the little stuff slide. Fight the battles worth fighting.

2. *Never tell someone they are wrong unless you are intending to irritate them.*

Even if you know someone is wrong on a fact they just stated, try to avoid telling them they are wrong. You can say you disagree, but don't say you are wrong. Explain your side of the argument and let them conclude for themselves they are wrong. It also leaves you an easy way out if you happen to be the one that is wrong.

I do not like to be told I am wrong, but if you present an intelligent counter argument I will quickly see your point and concede I was wrong. You win the argument and everyone leaves happy.

3. *Admit when you are wrong.*

I cannot tell you how many times I have seen someone continue to argue their point even though I can see in their eyes they know they are wrong. They are trying to leave the conversation with their self-respect intact so they continue to make ridiculous arguments in a desperate attempt to confuse others.

I have never seen this tactic work and it usually makes people doubt your intelligence and your integrity, which is not a good spot to be in. I took me a very long time to realize the joy and satisfaction I can bring others by admitting when I am wrong.

If you know you are wrong, readily admit it. People will respect you for it.

4. *Separate the messenger from the message.*

There are certainly people that annoy me in this world. When the opportunity presents itself, I might be tempted to point out where they might be incorrect on something. In fact, I might take great pleasure in it. At least for me, the reality is I would likely end up regretting it later, even if I was indeed right.

I refer you back to the first point, if it is not a battle worth fighting, leave it alone. Be the bigger person.

#76: Try not to burn bridges unnecessarily.

I think email is one of the more overused forms of communication. There are a lot of times email is not appropriate. For me personally, I think one of those inappropriate times is when you are changing jobs. I am not a big fan of the goodbye email.

In this age of downsizing and job hopping there are more opportunities to send a goodbye email than ever before. The funny thing is, there do not seem to be any hard and fast rules for the goodbye email.

I have seen a lot of versions of the goodbye email. The following are a few common types of goodbye emails I have seen over the years:

1. *The Positively Fictional Goodbye*

This is the email you get from the guy you know absolutely hated the company. From the day he started he has complained about everything. On his last day, he sends out a note expressing how wonderful the experience has been and how much he will miss everyone.

If you were truly miserable at a company, do not send an email expressing how great the experience was. It comes off as fake and insincere. A kind word on your final day will not make up for years of your complaining.

2. *The Parting Shot Goodbye*

These are perhaps the most entertaining of all of the goodbye emails, but they do far more harm than good, in my opinion. These are the notes where the soon to be departed takes a shot or several shots at management.

Sometimes the shot is covert, and you have to look for the hidden meaning in the words, but most times it is far more overt. What is the point of expressing your frustrations with management in an email to all of your coworkers on your last day? In the best case scenario, what good do you think will come of it? You gave the appropriate notice, you continued working diligently until your last day, and then you throw it all away by sending out your parting shot goodbye.

Hope that new job works out, because you certainly will not be able to come back to your old job, or use anyone from the company as a reference on your next job hunt.

3. *The Mass Goodbye*

This is a short and professional email, lacking any emotion that gets blasted to everyone in the company. If your company has less than ten people, maybe this is appropriate, but if you work in a large corporation, it is unlikely that everyone is going to care you are leaving. Many of the people you are going to send this to are simply going to delete it without even reading it. What's the point?

I am not against saying goodbye, but if you really want to do right, personalize it. My personal preference would be to make a list of everyone I need to say goodbye to and make time on my calendar to either speak to them in person or call them. As a last resort, I would send an email, but if I did it would be personalized and sent to only one person.

If someone is not worth taking two minutes to say goodbye, you probably don't need to say anything to them before you leave.

People tend to get bold and stupid when they are sending emails. They are much more confident than they would be if they were face to face. That confidence can cause you to send a poorly thought out email on your final day. Once it is out there, you can't get it back.

#77: Make a good first impression.

First impressions mean a lot. I doubt that is a revelation to you, but it is something I want you to spend a little time thinking about today. The first impression you make with someone can have a dramatic impact on how your relationship develops. I don't care if it is an employer or a potential dating partner, the first impression sets the tone for the relationship.

There are a few things I think you can do to increase the chances of making a good first impression:

1. Be on time.

For any meeting with anyone, I am of the impression you should do all you can to be on time. It is disrespectful to be late to a meeting. It implies your time is more important than others involved in the meeting (I point this fact out to my doctor every time I visit). Stuff happens to make you late, I get that. Believe me, I do. I still feel if you are consistently late to meetings, you need to make an adjustment.

Make your meeting a little shorter to give yourself more time. Try 45-minute meetings instead of an hour. The bottom line is it is important to be on time, but it is essential for your first meeting with someone.

2. Smile.

Don't underestimate the power of your smile. Smiling helps to put people at ease. It encourages positive interactions. Have you ever met someone that doesn't smile? How did it make you feel? Probably not good, I am guessing.

Take it from someone that does not smile a lot (I am working on it), smiling leaves a good impression on people.

3. Try not to talk too much.

When some people get nervous, such as when they are meeting someone new, they tend to talk a lot. If this description fits you, try to be aware of that and make a conscious effort to scale back your chatter.

If you want to make a good impression on someone, let them talk about themselves. Try not to fill every moment with nervous chatter.

4. *Be prepared for small talk.*

Now that I have told you not to talk so much, I will tell you that you need to be prepared to carry the conversation. This may seem like conflicting information, but it is not. It just depends on who you are meeting.

A lot of times, when I casually sit down with employees in my company, they are a little intimidated and it is hard to get them to talk. I am very good at small talk. I always do a quick read of the sports headlines. I don't watch baseball or car racing, but I can talk enough about them to draw someone out of their shell. Kids and pets are other great topics that can help people start talking.

Practice your small talk on friends and family. You never know when you might need it.

I am intentionally failing to list appearance, not because it is not crucial, but appearance is rather hard to define. The context of when, why, and who you are meeting dictates what your appearance should be. For an interview, I am a suit and tie kind of guy, but I can assure that does not seem to be the norm here in Florida. There are too many variables for me to give good advice on appearance.

#78: Communicate with your employees frequently.

Can you communicate too much with your employees? Maybe, but I doubt that is an issue many companies are dealing with. I think that a far more likely scenario is your company is not communicating enough. What formal channels of communication exist at your company today?

I am going to outline three formal channels of communication I would recommend. You may not have the ability to implement all three, unless you are the CEO, but I welcome your feedback either way.

1. *Quarterly All Company Meetings*

I would recommend at least once a quarter the CEO hosts a meeting where they can provide a state of the company address. Generally, as a rule, employees want to know if things are going well or if they are not going so well. Tell them. You don't necessarily have to get into a lot of financial details, but it is fairly easy to convey if the company is on track or not.

This is also a chance to let folks know about any new sales the company has made. I think most people want to take some pride in their company, so give them information to be proud of. If you just beat out five of your competitors to land a new client, let the people know that.

It is also a great time to recognize individuals or teams that have had exceptional performance over the last quarter. If you want to get really crazy, you can have employees send in questions they want answered ahead of time and then answer them at the meeting.

I really feel that it is important for the employees to hear directly from the CEO/President on a regular basis. I have worked places where I never met, heard from, or interacted with the CEO in any way. Does your company have all company meetings? If so, how often?

2. *One-on-One Meetings with Direct Reports*

These meetings are crucial. They should happen weekly. I like for these meetings to be follower driven. In a perfect world, your direct reports would come into the meeting with a list of questions and/or concerns they want your input on. They would give you an update on where they stand against their objectives and an update on any outstanding projects you have assigned to them.

Finally, you could raise any questions or concerns you have and assign any new projects you need. In a perfect world, that is how it would work.

If you are not currently conducting one-on-ones, you need to start. You are likely going to have to drive the meetings for a while until your employees get used to the format. It is their meeting. It is a guaranteed time each week they will have your undivided attention.

I schedule my one-on-ones for 30 minutes, but I try not to have another meeting backed up against them. Sometimes, they take five minutes, and other times, we go well over the 30 minute mark.

I keep a running list for each one of my direct reports. Things come up each day that may raise a concern for me; instead of calling them every time I have a thought, I write them down and hit them with the list all at once. It is a far more efficient use of time. Of course, if something comes up that needs immediate attention, I deal with it immediately, but most things are not an emergency.

The one-on-one provides a format for you and your employees to communicate. Only good things can happen when you have open communication, so I highly encourage you to try this practice if you are not already doing it.

3. *Internal Website*

Most companies these days have some kind of internal website or intranet for employee access. It is a great place to post general information all employees need to know. An example would be changes to policies or benefits that would be relevant to everyone. These issues may not require a formal meeting, but they still need to be communicated.

#79: Ask good questions.

I, and many others, have written about the importance of hiring the right person for a job. Depending on where you work, your ability to recruit and retain top talent may be the difference between success and failure. Since hiring is such an important part of a manager's job, I wanted to offer a few practical tips that may help you ensure you are indeed hiring the right person for the job.

1. *Know what you are looking for.*

You would think this point would go without saying, but that has not been my experience. I think that most managers tend to get caught up on the technical aspects of a job. In some cases, that may be okay. If I am hiring a programmer or engineer, for example, I certainly want to know they are capable of doing what I need them to do.

Don't get so caught up on the technical skills that you forget to determine the other things that may be relevant. I am not a micromanager. I will not dictate to my supervisors how to do their jobs, so I need people who are capable of analyzing data and making decisions. I, therefore, have questions I use to determine if an applicant is comfortable making independent decisions.

The more I can get them to talk about decisions they have made in the past, the more comfort I can get with their decision-making ability. Decision making is important to me based on my management style, but what is important to you? Are you asking the right questions to determine an applicant's suitability?

2. Use multiple interviewers.

I am a big fan of doing multiple interviews, especially for higher level positions. I have biases and you have biases, whether we want to admit to them or not. In many cases, I don't think we are even aware of our biases. Every human being has some sort of bias. Maybe I subconsciously like an applicant because he graduated from the same college that I went to. Maybe I subconsciously dislike a candidate because they worked for a company in which I once had a bad experience with. The list of things that can cause us to be biased in unlimited.

One way to try to alleviate the risk of biases is to conduct multiple interviews with different interviewers. Once the interviews are completed, the interviewers can compare notes and explain their reasons for liking or disliking applicants. If other interviewers really liked an applicant you did not, perhaps you need to consider what your biases might have been against that applicant.

3. Ask probing questions, and then keep digging.

I think that a lot of managers look for the "best" questions to ask interviewers. A good set of questions can certainly help you learn more about an applicant, but I think honing your ability to ask follow-up questions may be even more important. I will ask people to explain their duties at previous jobs and their reasons for leaving, but after that I tend to go with more open-ended questions. "Can you tell me the last time you had to deal with an irate customer? What made them irate? Were you able to resolve the situation, if so how? What leads you to believe that was the right course of action?"

There are no right answers to these questions, but rather they are designed to allow the applicant to talk about how they came to the decisions they did. It allows me to assess their decision-making skills. The key to this type of questioning is get clarification on anything not obvious to you. Keep asking clarification questions until you are sure exactly what decision-making steps they took to come to the conclusions they did. Your goal is to learn about their decision-making journey.

#80: Create a culture of civility.

I can be a little critical of leaders. I would like to believe my assessments are fair, but they can certainly be harsh. One thing that causes me to cast an instant negative judgment on a leader is if I see them walk by employees without acknowledging them. I realize today's workplace runs at a faster pace than it ever has at any time in our history, but that is no excuse for throwing civility out the window. I truly believe you have to lead by example, and I think the leader of a group sets the tone for civility. Incivility is contagious, especially when the leader is demonstrating it on a regular basis.

If you are a new manager starting out, don't underestimate the power of saying hello to your team each day. It helps to create a warm and caring atmosphere. Don't worry. I am not getting all touchy feely on you; there is practical value in my opinion. If I look back over the course of my career, I have had seven different jobs over the course of the last twenty or so years. Some of those jobs were very different than what I do now, and some were very similar. When I think back to the jobs I liked the most and the jobs I liked the least, I realize the actual job had very little to do with my overall happiness with the position. What caused me to like or dislike a job were the people I worked with and the culture that existed in the company.

The culture of a company is made up of many facets, but civility is darn sure one of them. I believe that incivility causes employees stress, anxiety, and perhaps even depression. I am not a psychiatrist, but I don't think I need to be one to come to the conclusion that when people walk by you like you don't exist, it has a negative impact on your self-esteem.

Again, I am not a doctor, but I am willing to bet that when you are stressed and depressed you tend to be absent far more. High absenteeism results in low morale. All of this has a negative impact on the company's ability to do whatever it is that they do.

How is the civility culture at your workplace? I think it is pretty good where I work, and I think that is part of the reason we are able to attract and retain good employees, even though we tend not to be the highest paying employer in the area.

If the civility culture of your workplace is broken, I assure you it can be fixed. It takes a dedicated effort from everyone, but that effort needs to start with the managers. If you are a manager, I think it is your responsibility to own the civility culture of your department. Start by practicing a little common courtesy yourself. I walk around every morning and say good morning to my folks and ask how they are. I have a sincere interest in them, but I also know that action is one of the little things that make a job worth coming into each day.

Don't be afraid to discuss civility with your employees. If you see them treating each other poorly, pull the perpetrator aside and discuss the impact of their actions.

When your employees see you leading by example and addressing poor behavior, I promise they will start to treat one another much better, even when you are not around.

#81: Seek common ground with those that you cannot stand to be around.

If you work in a small company with a handful of people you like, you should consider yourself very fortunate. I think the majority of employed people are far more likely to work in large companies where they may not necessarily like everyone they work with. What about you? Do any of your coworkers get under your skin on a regular basis?

I most assuredly work for a large company and I do not like everyone I work with. Fortunately for you, I have not liked a lot of people over the course of my career, so I can share a few tips on how to handle these uncomfortable relationships.

Before I get into the tips, I want to reassure you it is okay to not like every single person you work with. It is a big, diverse world out there. We are not all going to agree on everything, nor are we all going to like each other.

If you have a strong dislike for someone, that is okay. If you are pretty sure one of your coworkers has a strong dislike for you, that is okay too. The key is to ensure you can work professionally and effectively with everyone.

Here are a few other tips that may help you deal with bad work relationships.

1. Consider why.

If you have built up a strong dislike for a fellow employee, try to identify why you dislike them. Have they really earned your hatred or could you be the petty one in this relationship? This may not sound like groundbreaking advice, but trust me, it is. When you actually attempt to articulate your reasons for disliking someone, they may sound petty and silly to even you.

I can assure you I have personally experienced this on several occasions. When I tried to write out the reasons I disliked someone, I realized I was being childish and petty. It happens to the best of us.

2. Don't share your feelings with co-workers.

If we truly dislike one of our coworkers one of our first temptations is to tell our work friends. We need someone to share our frustrations with, right? There is no value is sharing your dislike. Even if they agree with you, it does not make you right, nor does it solve anything. If you want to speak to someone about the frustrations you are feeling, try speaking to the person you are having the issues with. (See point #3.)

3. Seek resolution.

If you notice a pattern of bad interactions with a coworker it may be time to confront the situation. Sit down with the person, and let them know what they are doing that causes you frustration. Give them the opportunity to explain their reasons for being frustrated with you as well.

I have had this type of meeting several times in the course of my career and they have never made the issues disappear completely, but the meetings have helped parties to be a little more cognizant of our actions and their impact. If you cannot resolve your issues, at least make sure both of you understand it is in your best interest to learn how to effectively work together. We certainly do not have to like each other, but we do need to be able to work together professionally.

#82: Deliver bad news promptly.

Few people will argue that trust is a major component in any successful relationship. I don't care if you are building relationships with your employees, your boss, or your spouse. Trust is a vital part of a healthy and productive relationship. I cannot imagine trying to run a successful company where the employees did not trust management and the managers had no trust in the employees.

Do you trust your manager? Do you trust in the management of your organization above your manager? I trust my manager. I am very thankful for that fact, as there have been times in my career I did not trust my manager and those have been the jobs I was the least happy. Yes, there is a correlation between trust and happiness. Do I trust the management above my manager? That is a more complex question. To some degree, but there have definitely been times I had a few doubts.

I think that one of the easiest ways to erode trust in a relationship is to withhold information. More specifically, withhold negative information. For instance, I have worked at companies that could not afford to give an annual pay increase to their employees. As hard as that is to tell employees, I think if you do it promptly and explain the reasons why, such as you are trying to keep from laying people off, you will be amazed at how well employees respond to this news. I have personally delivered this news and gotten a standing ovation from the employees I delivered it to. I delivered the news almost as soon as I got it and I explained exactly why we were doing it.

I have worked at other places that were not going to give an annual increase, and they delayed telling the employees anything for months. The increases were due in February, and the month passed with no increases and no word on when or if they were going to be paid or why. With no other information being provided to them, the employees started assuming why the increases were not being paid.

I started hearing things like management did not care about the employees, management was getting big bonuses, and we were about to shut the whole company down and go into bankruptcy. If no other information is being presented, people can get very creative with reasons why.

If you have bad news to deliver, I would urge you to do it swiftly. If you delay giving your employees bad news and they hear it from another source, your credibility gets hurt. Do it frequently, and you will have no credibility, or trust, with your employees.

This book is dedicated to improving the managerial skills of anyone that is kind enough to read it, but this is a lesson that transcends management. If you want to lose trust with anyone, delay giving them bad news. When they finally do get the news, they will start to make all kinds of assumptions on why you delayed telling them. Those assumptions will likely not be favorable to you.

Trust is funny that it can take a very long time to build up, but only a moment to lose. Don't delay in providing bad news to your employees, as it is a sure fire way to lose their trust.

HOW TO MANAGE YOURSELF BETTER

Are there things you fully intend to do, but in the back of your mind suspect you will never do? Good intentions will not make a good manager, execution will. They key to effective execution is managing yourself. Most managers overlook themselves when they are evaluating performance. Take a step back, and make sure you are performing at the optimal level.

#83: Focus on what is important.

What do you spend your time doing every workday? Have you ever left work wondering if you accomplished anything? I have certainly had days like that. I used to spend a lot of time answering emails. When I really looked at it, a lot of those emails did not have any value. The emails did not help my company to retain clients, bring on new clients, or enhance the client experience in any way.

I had an epiphany one day, and I started carving out a little time where I would not answer emails. I would shut down Outlook completely. Instead, I focused my thoughts and energy on how I could be a better manager. I looked at process flows, wrote development plans, and some days I would actually just sit and talk with my employees. I would have them show me what they do and ask their opinion how we could do things a little better.

The results were amazing! My department increased productivity, decreased costs and we have virtually eliminated turnover. The number of simple ideas my employees communicated to me was astounding. Good things happen when you stop answering email and start focusing on what is important.

#84: Follow a few tips for new managers.

I work with a young lady that was recently promoted into a management position in another department. I was mildly surprised to see she invited me and several other folks to a meeting this week. The meeting was scheduled for 30 minutes and there were a number of fairly senior people scheduled to attend. The topic was relevant to me, but as she was a brand new manager, I was very tempted to delegate this meeting to one of my managers. I pictured everyone coming into a room and the senior managers taking the meeting over in the absence of any true leadership. Fortunately for me, I forgot to delegate this meeting so I ended up going.

I walked into the meeting room about a minute ahead of time and there were four people already there, including the young lady running the meeting. I think there may have been two or three other people scheduled to attend, but clearly everyone was not there yet. Much to my surprise, this brand new manager started the meeting precisely on time. This alone would have impressed me, but it only got better.

Next, she handed out an agenda. She immediately started in on the purpose of the meeting. We were there to solve a problem several of our clients had expressed concern over. She stated the facts, what she perceived to be the root cause, and launched into her proposed solution.

She had clearly spent a great deal of time preparing for this meeting. I thought her analysis was impeccable, and her solution was exactly what I would have prescribed. She was simply informing us of the solution and looking for our blessing. She quickly received everyone's blessing and promptly ended the meeting, fourteen minutes after it had started.

With my extra sixteen minutes, I went back to my desk and shot her an email letting her know how impressed I was with the way she conducted the meeting.

If you are a new manager, there are several lessons you can learn here, such as the following:

1. Don't bring your manager problems; bring them solutions.

If you are a new manager and you want to quickly stand out, when you discover a problem do a little research so you can propose a solution. When you bring a problem to your manager, you should be bringing at least one proposed solution.

I literally have dozens of people telling me problems every day. I have very, very few that offer solutions. If you want to make a name for yourself quickly, this is the way to go.

2. Start meetings on time.

If you start and end meetings on time, you will find people will start to come to the meetings on time. This showing up five minutes late for every meeting is a learned behavior. We do it because we know the meetings are not going to start on time. I also tend to accept meetings more often from people I know will end them early.

3. *Have an agenda for your meeting.*

Have an agenda for your meeting. (Oops! I said that twice. I guess it must be important.) If you are a new manager, most senior managers will assume you do not know what you are doing yet. Whether it is true or not, that is the assumption they will make.

One very easy way to refute that assumption is to provide tangible evidence that you know exactly what you will be doing for the next sixty minutes. Give them an agenda. An agenda gives you instant creditability. It also shows everyone involved you respect their time. Most importantly, it helps keep the meeting on point.

Some folks like to hear themselves talk. They start going off on a tangent. The agenda helps you keep them focused. It also provides the un-prepared people in the meeting something to take notes on. Yes, I still see people come to meetings all the time with nothing to write on. I guess they have better memories than I do.

#85: Set your goals a little bit higher.

Do you know who Sister Madonna Buder is? She is probably one of the most inspirational people I have ever heard of. At the tender young age of 75, she became the oldest woman to compete in and complete an Ironman Triathlon.

For those of you not triathletes, an Ironman triathlon is made up of a 2.4 mile swim, followed by a 112 mile bike, and then they cap it off with a 26.2 mile run. To complete one requires perseverance, planning, initiative, and incredible time management skills. To complete an Ironman at the age of 75 is beyond my ability to comprehend.

I have completed several half Ironmans (1.2 mile swim, 56 mile bike, and 13.1 mile run), but I have yet to take on the challenge of a full Ironman. Honestly, I am afraid of the time commitment required for the 8-9 months leading up to the event.

A lot of people I know think I am crazy for running triathlons, marathons, and most recently a Tough Mudder, but exercise is the only way I can keep off excess weight, and if I am going to exercise I want to make it as fun as possible. Training for these events makes it fun and challenging. It also keeps me committed. There are many days I do not feel like running, but I know I have an event coming up and cannot afford to miss a training day. Maybe it is my frugal nature, but once I sign up for a race and send in my money—most of these types of races can be pricey—I am going to complete it.

I have only failed to complete one race and that was my first attempt at a marathon. It had nothing to do with failing to train, but everything to do with failing to plan. It's a long story that we will save for another day.

Are you impressed with Sister Madonna Buder? Don't be. I have not told you the best part yet. After becoming the oldest person to complete the Ironman in 2005, she went on to break her record of being the oldest person to complete the race several more times. Her most recent record breaking effort was last year. She completed the Ironman in less than 17 hours at the age of 81.

She has already announced her intention to compete this year at age 82. I forgot to mention one other thing; she did not start any type of training until she was 48. She began training as a way to achieve relaxation and calmness. From there she built up her endurance to run her first Ironman at the age of 55, and she has kept running them since.

What goal can you set for yourself this year? After learning about an 82 year old nun that can out swim, out bike and easily outrun me, it may be time for me to reassess whether I am setting my goals high enough. Your goals do not have to be fitness related. Is there a degree you want to pursue, a skill you want to learn? It's never too late. All you need is a little inspiration, a goal, and a plan. Hopefully I helped you with the first one.

#86: Treat everyone like the CEO.

Have you ever known someone that would be sweet and nice as they could be with the boss, but a complete jerk to everyone else? I have seen a few people like this over the course of my career and I have detested each one of them.

I do not appreciate people that have two sets of manners; one for those above them on the corporate ladder and one for those below. It sends a very clear message to those below that they are not important, and certainly not as important as the people above you.

My advice is to treat everyone as if they were the CEO of your organization. If you wouldn't send a snide email to your CEO, don't send it to a coworker.

You never know how your organization may change and who you may be reporting to in the future. It is best to not annoy the heck out of people that may eventually be your boss. Treat everyone nicely and you will never have to worry about who your next boss will be.

#87: Know that "busy" does not mean "effective."

In my twenty years of leadership I have learned a simple truth that has proven to have very few exceptions. People that talk about how busy they are on a consistent basis, are generally not the most effective people in your organization. The people who talk the most about being busy are generally the ones that are the most insecure about how little they are actually getting done.

A lot of times they are not necessarily unproductive because they are lazy—although I have seen a few cases that did involve laziness— but rather, they are unproductive. There is motion and action, but very little is accomplished.

I think there are a number of reasons for this, such as the following:

1. *They take on too much.*

I know people who will not say no to any meeting request. They will attend any meeting they are invited to, whether it is relevant to them or not. I am not that guy. I have no problem turning down meeting requests.

You may think you are not high enough in the organization to engage in this sort of behavior, but I have made a career of turning down meeting requests. If I am not sure I can add anything to a meeting, or if a meeting is not going to accomplish anything, I tend to decline it. If you spend all day in meetings, you cannot be shocked when you are not accomplishing anything.

2. *They failure to prioritize.*

I have talked about this before, and will likely talk about it in the future. If you only use a to-do list to determine what you are going to do, you are never going to maximize your efficiency. A to-do list is a great start, but it will not get the job the done. You will gravitate to the easiest things to do on your list. Very rarely are they the things that have the biggest payback.

They are not the task that will make you successful. I keep a to-do list every day, but I prioritize that list.

I work first on things that will make the biggest difference in my life. Do the things that have the biggest payback first. In many cases, you will find they are the ones you least want to do.

3. *They have unrealistic self-expectations.*

I am pretty good at estimating how long it will take me to do certain things. If anything, I tend to err on the side of caution and estimate a task may take a little longer than it actually does. Not everyone has this gift. I know people who regularly fail to estimate their time correctly, and as a result, they over promise things and take on way more work than they should.

As a result this, they always feel stressed about things they have to do. I don't know if this is an issue for you or not, but I bet that you do.

4. *They mistake action for effectiveness.*

I know several people I work with that I believe define themselves by how busy they are. If they are busy, they must be important and valuable to the organization. None of my clients know how busy I am. None of my clients know how busy anyone on my team is. All of my clients know we get results.

I am pretty sure that is what creates job security. If I make my clients happy, and take care of my employees, I will consider myself a smashing success, even if I am not running around like crazy each day.

Without sounding too arrogant (I will let you be the judge of that), I can say I am one of the most effective people I know. I see a lot of people each and every day that are far busier than I, but not nearly as effective.

If you feel you are extremely busy, but not actually accomplishing anything, I would try to focus on the four points I list above. I am confident you may be guilty of at least one of them.

#88: Learn how to take a compliment.

How well do you take a compliment? If your boss praises you in front of a group, how does that make you feel?

I hate it, and I have never been good at receiving compliments. As bad as I am at receiving negative feedback, I think I take it much better than I take positive feedback. I don't think I am alone in this. I think there are a large number of people do not how to take a compliment. Are you one of them?

Like any bad habit, I am out to correct this. I have done a little research, I have conducted a few social experiments, and I am now ready to share my conclusions. With no further ado, here is my advice on how to take a compliment.

1. Don't discredit yourself.

Don't tell people you do not deserve their praise, or say, "Oh, it was nothing." Not only is it damaging to you—if you tell me enough times you do not deserve it, I may start to believe it—it is disrespectful to the person giving you the compliment. They felt strongly enough about your performance to reach out and let you know it. If you have faith in their judgment, be gracious and accept the compliment. Just say, "Thank you."

2. Don't question their intentions.

I will be the first to admit I am skeptical when someone pays me a compliment. I have learned painfully through experience, they do not always have a secret motive for giving me a compliment. In fact, very rarely have I found their motives were anything other than acknowledging what I had done.

If you have no reason to doubt the person giving you the compliment, be gracious and accept the compliment. Just say, "Thank you!"

3. Sharing the credit is okay, but recognize you were a part of the success as well.

Don't say, "My team really deserves all of the credit," unless you truly did nothing. If you played a role in the success, a better response may be, "Thank you for your kind words, and I would also like to thank my team for their contributions to this success."

It is okay to accept a compliment for your contribution, especially if you are acknowledging the others that contributed. This does not feel natural at all to me, but I do think it is okay to accept a compliment for your part of a team project.

4. It is okay to acknowledge the appreciator.

I have had so many people tell me they do not believe their boss appreciates what they do. If the day comes where your boss does appreciate you, make sure you acknowledge that.

You could say, "Hey, I really appreciate you taking the time to acknowledge the work I did for the new client. It means a lot to me, thanks." It encourages this type of behavior in the future. Even bosses need a little feedback.

#89: Don't be that person.

One of the downsides to working in a large corporation is you encounter a large number of people each day. If you have a large enough group, there are bound to be a few folks that might pluck your nerves.

I would like to believe I am tolerant of all of the folks I work with. I try to learn from each of them, even the ones that may annoy me. Everyone is capable of teaching us something. At the very least, these folks have taught me a few character traits I know I need to be mindful of if I don't want to become "that guy." You know, the one people simply don't want to be around.

It does not matter where you work. If you are in a large enough organization, I am sure you have some of the following people in your office:

1. Mr. Negativity

Every place I have ever worked has had at least one person that can find the negative side of just about anything. If the company announced they were going to give a thousand dollar bonus to each employee, this guy would complain they are going to take more taxes out of his check. If you buy lunch for the office, he will not like the food. He disagrees with any promotions or changes in company policies. Do you have this guy in your office?

It is especially tough if this guy is in a leadership position, because his negativity will rub off on his entire team. I can't stand to be around negative people. I find them emotionally draining—though they have taught me very valuable lessons.

Just as you can find a negative side to just about anything, you can also find a positive side. Look for the positive and embrace it. If something is truly that bad, find a way to fix it. Just sitting around and complaining will not solve anything and may just make you the guy, or gal, people do not want to be around.

2. Mrs. Drama

Sorry, ladies, I picked on the guys for the first one, so I am just trying to even it out. Have you ever worked with someone who shared just about every aspect of their personal lives with the whole office? You get to hear each personal call they have, because they speak loud enough for the whole office to hear when they are yelling at their kids or spouse on the phone. In case you miss any part of the call, they will recap the whole thing for everyone when they get off of the phone. You get to hear it all: calls with their doctor, bill collectors, teachers, or maybe a probation officer if you are really lucky.

Just for the record, I have seen men and women that fall into this category. These folks have taught me it is best to keep personal matters personal. Some of the conversations I have overheard have made me, and everyone in earshot, uncomfortable.

I don't want to be this type of person, and fortunately it is not difficult to avoid this scenario. If you work in a small office where people can easily overhear your calls, step outside at lunch time and make your personal calls on your cell phone.

3. Mr. Validation

I have worked with a number of people who seem to need constant validation and praise. Don't get me wrong. I like to give praise often to those that deserve it, but some folks can't seem to get enough of it. They are constantly updating you with their latest achievements and patiently waiting for you to rain down praise upon them. It is not feedback that they want; it is praise. If you happen to have occasion to give them a little constructive feedback, they are distraught for days.

Those of you that work in small offices may think I am exaggerating this point. I assure you I am not. I could tell you stories related to this point that would make you laugh and cry at the same time.

I appreciate when my boss acknowledges the work that I do, but I have learned to not go looking for that acknowledgement. Just be pleasantly surprised when it happens. Don't get to the point that you are expecting it or waiting for it.

#90: When times get tough, don't micromanage.

If you are a mid or senior level manager, you will eventually get to a point that you have to make a very critical decision. Times will get tough and you will be faced with delegating responsibility, or taking it on yourself. I have seen managers face this dilemma hundreds of times, and the tendency is always managers take on more and more responsibility as times get tougher.

In my world I see this often when it comes to hiring decisions and overtime approval. When sales are down, one of the first things I see happen is basic decision-making starts gets pushed to higher and higher levels. When the money is flowing in, managers are given guidance on hiring and left to make their own hiring decisions. When the revenues are down, suddenly a manager that has previously made impeccable hiring decisions now has to go to their manager to get approval on their hiring decisions. As revenues go down even further, that approval get pushed higher and higher in the organization until eventually the CEO is making all of the hiring decisions.

I have seen this exact scenario play out dozens of times, and I have seen it cover much more than just hiring decisions. I have seen this logic used to make decisions on the use of overtime, selecting vendors, or even buying basic office supplies.

Have you seen this scenario play out in your organization? I understand the logic behind it, but I certainly don't agree with it. The logic is, as the decision-making gets pushed up, people will get intimidated or frustrated by the bureaucracy and will make fewer requests. Fewer requests for new employees, overtime, and office supplies all can help to reduce your operating expenses. That is exactly what you want to do when revenues down, right? Maybe, but probably not, in my opinion. What if that hour of overtime would help to retain a large client, but the manager is too frustrated by the bureaucracy to even ask? Yes, you reduced expenses, but at what cost?

If revenues are down, then I think the CEO and other senior managers have a responsibility to reduce expenses accordingly. They have a responsibility to create a vision, of lower expenses in this case and they need to ensure the vision is clearly communicated to each of their managers. Their managers in turn need to communicate the vision to their departments and formulate plans to achieve the vision. If the CEO's vision is to reduce expenses by 20% by the end of the quarter, they need to communicate that vision and reward those that hit the goal, and coach and/or replace those that do not, depending on how many times they have previously failed to hit goal).

Am I over simplifying this? It does not seem difficult to me and it really only requires a little communication.

Here is the best part: If the senior managers are not spending all of their time deciding whether or not employees should get a new stapler, they are free to focus on building new revenue. Wasn't that the problem in the first place? If we go out there and generate enough new revenue, everybody can get a new stapler.

#91: Be a good (cubicle) neighbor.

I have worked in an office environment my entire adult life. This means I have been surrounded by cubicles my entire adult life, which in turn means I have seen thousands of breeches of cubicle etiquette. What is cubicle etiquette, you ask?

Cubicle etiquette is a commonly accepted set of unwritten rules that the majority of your coworkers are going to follow and expect you to follow. Failure to do so can slow your career progression, alienate your coworkers, and literally cause people to hate you.

Here are a few of the basic rules of cubicle etiquette.

1. Pay attention to non-verbal cues.

If you stop by my cubicle and I fail to look up at you when you start talking, I am busy and do not want to be interrupted. Politely excuse yourself, and let me know that you will stop back later to tell me whatever important thing you need to tell me. If I don't look up at you, don't keep talking. Not only am I not listening to you, but you are mildly irritating me. No eye contact means you should keep moving.

2. *Speakerphones and cubicles don't mix.*

If you are sitting in a cubicle and do not have an office door that closes you off from the rest of the world, you should never use a speakerphone, even if you are only checking voicemail. It is disruptive to everyone around you. I don't feel the need to explain this one in a lot of detail; just don't do it.

3. *Don't make or receive personal calls from your cubicle.*

Your coworkers do not want to hear you making your next doctor's appointment, and they certainly don't want to hear the reason you are making it. If you have to make a personal call, step into a conference room or step outside.

I do not make or receive a lot of personal phone calls during the day and I have a very difficult time understanding people who do. I come to work to work, and that is where my focus is while I am there. On the flip side, I also do not get a lot of calls from work when I am at home.

Practice a little work life balance, and try to keep your personal life out of the workplace.

4. *Be careful with décor.*

It is certainly okay to add your personal touch to your cubicle, but you can easily overdo it. If you are going to display pictures, try to ensure that they are appropriate for the workplace. The picture of you winning the booty shaking contest during spring break in college is likely a great conversation starter, but it is probably not appropriate for the office.

Plants are another pet peeve of mine. Done in moderation they are fine, but don't bring in too many plants, or plants that are too large for the space. Plants can be messy and they can also attract insects. Don't be the crazy plant person.

5. *Don't share your music.*

If you are going to listen to music at work, use headphones. If you are using headphones, do not turn your music up so loud that I can easily determine what song you are listening to when I walk by.

Even if those around you say they don't mind if you listen to your music without headphones, don't do it. They are just being polite.

6. *Think twice before eating at your desk.*

Before you unwrap that garlic and onion sandwich, think about the impact the smell is going to have on your neighbors. Try to eat your meals away from your cubicle. Food smells can linger for hours after you are finished eating.

7. *Don't "borrow" things from other cubicles.*

How annoying is it when you go to staple something and your stapler is not where it is supposed to be? It then becomes your highest priority to find it. You spend the next fifteen minutes searching for it only to realize that your cubicle neighbor "borrowed" it.

Try to not borrow things when your neighbors are not in their cubes. If you absolutely must borrow something, return it.

8. *Obey the dress code.*

My company has a dress code. There are people that like to push the limits of the dress code. I notice them, and I can't help but form judgments about them based on their poor fashion choices.

If your manager has to take time out of their day to call you into a room to remind you of the dress code, do you think that has a positive impact on your career progression?

I openly encourage employees to try and stand out in many different ways, but dressing provocatively or poorly is not the way to separate you from the crowd.

9. *Keep it neat.*

A completely disorganized cube with stacks of papers sends a very bad message to those around you, even when you are not at work.

10. Obey the Golden Rule.

As a general rule, if it bothers you when other people do something at their cube, avoid doing the same in your cube.

#92: Develop your grit.

I think most people realize there are very few "overnight" success stories. Oprah Winfrey did not become a media mogul overnight. Bill Gates did not become the most epic programmer in the world overnight. Michael Jordan did not become the most prolific basketball player ever in a single evening. Their success was likely caused by a variety of characteristics, but one characteristic that they all shared was grit. There has been a lot written about grit of late. It is suddenly very vogue to be gritty.

So do you have grit? Grit is the ability to commit to long term goals, and the ability to maintain focus on those goals in the face of difficulty. Can you be the next Oprah, Bill Gates or Michael Jordan? I don't think genetics has a whole lot to do with it, so I guess the answer is yes, you can. Before you start looking for an agent to represent you, there is one other factor to consider.

According to Malcolm Gladwell in his book *Outliers*, it takes about 10,000 hours to become an expert in something. That's 10,000 hours of practicing your interview skills, 10,000 hours of programming, or 10,000 hours perfecting your dunk. I think this is where most people fail in their quest to be a superstar. We start out with every intention of devoting our life to an endeavor, but then we are distracted and we never get anywhere close to that 10,000 hour mark. How well you are able to handle distractions and obstacles is what determines just how gritty you are.

I would like to develop my grit, but I am not quite sure how to go about that. There are no grit development courses I am aware of. I think if you want to be grittier, you are on you own. So let's say I want to be the world's greatest blogger and I am prepared to commit to 10,000 hours of blogging to develop my expertise. How do I increase my chances of being the world's greatest blogger?

1. Define the objective.

Being the world's greatest blogger is probably a little vague. It is pretty subjective. I could say I am the world's greatest blogger tomorrow if I believed that. We want to have a more tangible definition. To make this easy we will define it as have more daily traffic on my blog than any other blogger. So now that I have defined it, I need to write it down. Always write your goals down.

2. Define the necessary actions.

To keep this simple, I will say to achieve my goal I need to develop my ability to write original material, and I need to research other blogs to determine what works and what does not work. I want to devote two hours a day to each of these activities. Once I have decided on the necessary actions and the amount of time I can afford to allot to each activity, I just need to write it down—on a calendar, that is. I would plot two hours for each activity into my daily planner. So far, so good.

I think everyone is capable of doing the first two very enthusiastically. So where are we likely to fail? On #3.

3. Do it.

Now I have a plan and I have my action items scheduled each day, I just need to do it. In this case, I need to spend two hours writing and two hours researching each day. It sounds simple enough.

The problem is that at some point I am going to get distracted by life. Kids get sick; I may not feel "creative" at the appointed time; or I just might not feel like writing today. There are two factors that will work against you here.

The first is self-control. I have never spoken with Michael Jordan, but I feel very confident in saying I am sure that there were days he did not feel like playing basketball. It may have taken a little extra self-motivation on those days, but he still went out there and practiced.

The other factor that works against you is self-confidence. Most of us don't believe we can be exceptional. You may have believed it when you were a kid, but somewhere along the line you lost it. People love to tell you what you can't do, and at some point, you start to believe them.

It is easier to be mediocre. It requires a lot less effort and gives you plenty of free time for television. So on those days you don't feel like writing, you can rationalize not writing by telling yourself you would never finish the book anyway.

So if you want to develop your grit, you need to focus on two things. Exercising a little self-control and developing a little self-confidence.

I am going to try and help you with your self-confidence. Sometimes all we need to know is someone believes in us. Well, I believe in you, and I believe you are capable to doing whatever you set your mind to. I will share my rationale, so you don't think I am just saying that.

You are here reading this book. I do not write about celebrities or sports. I write about relatively dry topics: management and leadership. If you are here reading this, I have to believe that you have a sincere interest in bettering yourself. That fact alone makes you exceptional. Most people don't have that inner drive.

People that lack grit simply don't believe they have the same abilities as successful people. If you believe that, you are wrong. Planning, effort, and persistence are what you need to succeed.

There will be bad days you don't do what you needed to do. Shake them off and refocus. You only fail when you stop trying.

#93: Read outside of your area of expertise.

I tend to read books on leadership and management a lot. It keeps me current in the field and often inspires my own creative thoughts. There is absolutely nothing wrong with that, but be careful you are not limiting yourself to just your area of expertise.

I am not a salesperson. That is not my area of expertise. I have, however, learned a great deal from reading books on the art of selling. To some extent we are all sales people, as we have to sell ourselves and our ideas every day. Even beyond that, I have learned a lot about management from learning about how some organizations incentivize, recruit, and retain their sales people.

A manager can develop breakthrough ideas by learning what works in other fields. Don't limit yourself to reading about topics you already know or have the greatest interest in. Try to read on other topics outside of your area of expertise to develop a well-rounded management style.

#94: Be frugal when travelling for business.

At one point in my career, I traveled every week. Traveling is fun and exciting when you are a young man, but the novelty has definitely worn off for me. Fortunately, I don't travel nearly as often now, but I still probably hop on a plane at least once a month.

Your company may have policies around traveling that dictate which flights you can take, or how much you can spend on meals. My company has a travel policy which, to be completely honest, I have never read. That may sound strange coming from me. You might be thinking, *How can you enforce and adhere to a policy that you have never read?* That is a fair question, and I have a very good answer. When traveling, I spend money as if it were own. I don't go to five-star steakhouses. I don't run up $1000 bar tabs, and I certainly don't charge golf games to the company. I don't and nor do my employees. That is not the way I operate.

I have seen a lot of executives who regularly use their travel time as an opportunity to try out the finest hotels, eat at the finest restaurants, and run up bar tabs. I would be horrified to be associated with them. I am not sure at what level one starts to feel like they are entitled to be treated like a king at the company's expense, but apparently, I have not reached that level yet. When I see people do this, it leaves a very bad impression on me and one that I am not likely to forget.

At every moment in every workday, people are judging you. Your peers are judging you, your employees are judging you, and your boss is certainly judging you. Running up large and frivolous travel expenses is a great way to undermine any great work that you do. Nothing screams louder that you could care less about the company than running up large travel expenses. Is that the message you want to send?

Of all of the people I have seen abuse the travel policy with my current company, none of them are still with the company. I am not saying they got fired or laid off because of their travel habits, but I am confident it was at least one part of their demise.

For those of you in leadership positions, you have to consider the message you are sending when you run up frivolous travel expenses. That sends a very dangerous message to your employees about how important it is to control expenses.

If you are just starting your career out, I have a very simple piece of advice for you. Always spend your company's money as if it were you own. I don't care if everyone else in your company spends ridiculous amounts of money on travel. You need to be better than that. You need to be smarter than that.

The money you save will likely ultimately save jobs when times are lean. One of the jobs you save may be your own.

#95: Check your logic on big decisions.

Our minds can play tricks on us. I literally see it every day. We all can make some very irrational decisions based on shaky logic. I was guilty of it yesterday, which got me thinking about some of the shaky logic I have seen managers use.

Here are a few examples that popped into my mind, but I am curious to see if you have any to add to the list.

1. Polar Extremes

Things are either great or absolutely horrible. An employee's performance is either perfect or horrible and will not be tolerated.

When making decisions be careful with either/or type logic—especially when making personnel decisions. Employees are rarely perfect or perfect failures. The reality is they fall somewhere in between, so try to catch yourself when you using extremes in decision making.

2. Overgeneralization

I have seen many managers jump to a false conclusion with little or no data to support their decision. Sales are bad, so you conduct a training session for your sales people. The next day, you have a new sale. Problem solved right? A very wise man once told me one point does not make a trend, but I have seen many a manager try to argue that very point. When faced with a problem, they cling to the first piece of positive data they get and start to rejoice that they have solved the problem. Celebrate the battles you win, but never lose focus on winning the war.

3. Needing to Be Right

I know I am guilty of going to great extremes to prove I am right on a particular issue. It is almost as if someone is keeping score and I need to prove I was right to get that point. No one is keeping score, and sometimes proving that you were right can do far more damage than actually being wrong.

Before you set out to prove you are correct on something, consider what the benefits are going to be of convincing others you are right. Is it going to save a life, save a job, or just save your pride?

I know I am guilty of arguing points just to save my pride. If doing so comes at the expense of the feelings of those around me, what am I accomplishing?

If the fight is not worth fighting, then don't. Be wrong, even when you are right.

4. Believing in "Common Sense"

There is no such thing as common sense. What you consider to be common sense is a conglomeration of theories and conclusions you have come to, based on your life's experiences. My life's experiences will not match your experiences, so I will not have come to all of the same conclusions.

I have coached managers hundreds of times on this. They are frustrated with an employee because they come in late every day, so I will ask them if they have informed the employee of their expectation to arrive on time. I usually get the response, "They know they are supposed to be on time, that's common sense."

Maybe at their last job they could be a few minutes late and it was not a big deal. Maybe they concluded on the first time they were late that it was okay because no one said anything to them. The only way they will know it is not acceptable behavior is if you tell them.

There is no such thing as common sense. The sooner managers realize that, the better off they will be.

#96: Be someone worth being around.

I make a conscious effort to avoid negative people. I don't want them around me. Their negativity drains me and the next thing you know I start to take on their negative tendencies. I try to go the opposite direction and surround myself with upbeat people that will inspire me to step out of my comfort zone.

It is a good practice and one I recommend that you follow, but my question is this: Are you someone I would want to surround myself with?

There are certain people in this world you want to be around. They are charismatic; they make you feel good about yourself and your potential; and you are generally just happy being around them. Are you one of those people?

I spent a lot of time thinking about the people I like to be around and how I can make sure I am someone others want to be in the same radius with. The following is what I have come up with:

1. *Live life outside of work.*

I travel a lot. I participate in long distance triathlons, marathons, and I have also done a few obstacle course type races, like Tough Mudder. All of these things give me interesting stories when I need to make small talk with employees or clients. These stories help to make me interesting to other people.

No one is fascinated by what television shows you watched last night. Get out there on the weekends, and come back with a few stories of your own.

2. *Be curious.*

Ask people about things they are working on or the challenges they are facing. Give them a chance to talk about themselves a bit. Actually listen to what they are saying, and ask follow up questions.

3. *Share the things that you are happy about.*

No one wants to be around the person that is constantly complaining and unhappy about everything in their life. Be the person that is genuinely happy and spreading joy wherever you go.

In a nutshell, you need to apply the Golden Rule. Be the person you would like to be around.

#97: Study the true meaning of networking.

I think many people completely misunderstand the concept of networking. As a young man starting out in corporate America, many people advised me to never burn bridges and keep in contact with all the people I built relationships with. That advice was wasted on me, as I knew I was on the fast track to a corner office and would always be able to find a new job if I needed, as my resume would be impeccable. After twenty years of working, I am now starting to realize how important networking is.

I would like to share with you a few thoughts I have on the concept of networking, and I would like to hear your thoughts on the concept of networking as well.

1. *It is not about you.*

Your goal in networking should be to help other people. Yes, ideally people will want to help you as well, but your focus should be on how you can help others. This requires you really get to know the people in your network and understand their needs. What are the biggest problems they are facing? Can you help them solve any of their problems? Can you introduce them to someone who may be able to help them solve their problems?

You need to understand their needs before you ever start talking about your needs. Would you be more likely to help someone who has helped you in the past? I certainly would.

Review your list of contacts in LinkedIn today. Who can you help on that list? Not sure? Start reaching out to people you have not talked to in over a year and see what is going on in their lives. What obstacles are they facing? Remember, the fact you reached out to someone and made contact with them certainly does not put them in your debt. Reach out to people with sincere curiosity.

2. *It is about quality, not quantity.*

There is no need to "force" a connection with every single person you meet. You do not need to shotgun LinkedIn requests to every person you ever pass in a hallway. My thoughts on networking are the same as my thoughts on marketing my blog. I would rather have ten people following me that actually read what I write and get value from it, than a thousand people who just hit the site each day to put a comment in that promotes their site.

With networking, I would rather have three people in my network that would actually help me if I needed it, than five hundred that could care less if I needed help. Numbers don't mean anything. I am not impressed with people who have five hundred plus LinkedIn contacts. If you want to impress me, be an impressive person.

3. Don't dismiss people as irrelevant.

I was chatting about networking with an executive type gentleman, and he explained he generally did not accept LinkedIn requests from people he thought were not in a position to help him. While I understand the concept of wanting to get the most value for your networking time, I am not sure I understand how you could possibly determine who would be in a position to help you.

Anyone may be able to help you, or introduce you to someone who could help you. They may not be able to help you today, but you do not know what problems you will face tomorrow. I am happy to network with anyone I believe has a sincere interest in me.

#98: Don't waste time hating your job.

I am fortunate. I do not hate my job. I do not dread Monday mornings. I know not everyone is as fortunate as I, and I do not take my fortune for granted. I have spoken with a lot of people over the years in jobs they hate. Every situation is different, but I do think there are few pieces of advice I can list here that may be of benefit to anyone who currently hates their job:

1. You control your destiny.

If you don't like where you are in life, make a plan to get you to where you want to be. What field do you want to work in? What qualifications will you need for your dream job? How can you get those qualifications?

If you don't like where you currently are, you are going to have to start doing things a little differently. What are you going to start doing differently? Make a plan. Prioritize searching for a new job or enhancing your skills. Cut a little television time out, and work on things that are going to help you to change your situation.

2. Get a grip.

There are very few situations in which I would advocate quitting your current job when you do not have another position already lined up. It is a tough job market, and finding a new job may take longer than you think.

Devote as much time as you can to finding a new job, but do not quit your current job until you have something else lined up. I have made this mistake, and I have seen countless others do it as well. Do not make a stupid decision based on your emotional response to a bad day.

There have been jobs I wanted to leave, where my situation changed dramatically while I was trying to find a new job, and I ultimately ended up staying. Do not overreact to your current situation. Unless you are being asked to do something illegal or immoral, try to hold on to the job you have until you have a better alternative.

3. Make sure you are not the problem.

Look at those around you. Do they hate their jobs? If you are the only one miserable, the problem may be you. If that is the case, finding a new job may not solve the problem.

No one thinks they are the problem, but try to look at your situation as objectively as possible. Only you can decide if you are in the right job or not. You cannot listen to the advice of family or friends. It is a decision you have to make, but you need to at least be logical enough to realize you could be part of the problem.

4. Social Media is not the place to vent your frustration.

I don't even feel like I should have to explain this one, but I will. Your boss and your coworkers use the internet as well. Do not post your frustrations on Facebook or Twitter, or any social media platform.

You know what is worse than quitting a job before you have something else lined up? Getting fired from one before you have something else lined up. Google the words "fired over Facebook" if you need examples.

#99: Let go of grudges.

I can hold grudge. I can hold a grudge better than anyone I know. I am not saying that out of pride, but rather I want to ensure you understand I am an authority on this particular issue. If I perceive you have wronged me, I will not forget it. I am not sure if my inability to forgive is something I am looking to change or not.

Would you consider yourself to be a forgiving person, or are you someone that never forgets when you have been crossed?

We have all been hurt by other people. Whether the damage caused is intentional or accidental, personal or professional, at some point we are going to feel emotionally harmed by someone. Should we store that information away so we can protect against the same thing happening in the future, or should we truly try to forgive others?

Holding on to a grudge can have a negative impact on your relationships. That anger can carry over into your communications with other people, and before you know it, they are holding a grudge against you. We can easily get caught in a cycle of anger and hurt that can greatly hamper our ability to lead, or even maintain, a productive work environment.

If you Google the words "holding onto a grudge," you will find a couple of thousand sites that will advocate you learn to forgive and let go of any ill feelings you have. I could not find any sites advocating holding on to your grudge as a learning opportunity to protect against the same sort of thing happening in the future. I really looked hard for a site that would advocate that you should hold on to and learn from your anger, but I couldn't find it.

This left me an in interesting position. Apparently, I need to learn to let grudges go and forgive, but I have no idea how to do that. Like any dilemma I am faced with, I researched it and came up with a plan, which I am now going to share with you.

The following are three easy steps about how to forgive:

1. Understand the meaning of the word.

Make sure you understand what forgiving is. I think I may have gotten tripped here. To forgive someone does not condone their behavior. You are not excusing their behavior, but rather you are not holding onto the anger, frustration, and shock for something you ultimately cannot control.

2. Rationalize.

I am a very logical person, so it is easy for me to do the cost/benefit analysis on most decisions. There is no benefit to holding on to anger. It is unlikely that being angry is going to have a positive change on the person you are angry with. What's in for you? You can learn from the experience without holding onto your anger. If there is no value in an activity, don't engage in it.

3. Make a decision to move on with your life.

This is easier said than done, it requires the completion of the first two steps and a little willpower. I suspect this step may require some additional research to accomplish successfully, but I won't know until I try.

#100: Don't compare yourself to others.

I coach a lot of people. I coach them on professional issues and occasionally on personal issues. Based on my very limited experiences, it appears many people will artificially create unhappiness in their lives. They do this by comparing themselves to someone else.

I have seen people that were on top of the world compare themselves to someone else, only to come to the conclusion their life sucks. Sometimes that transformation can happen in only a few minutes. It has always amazed me at how destructive comparing yourself to others can be.

Do you know anyone that engages in this sort of behavior on a regular basis? They are people that cannot derive any joy from the success of others. When someone gets an award, they immediately start thinking about why it was not them to receive the award. If a co-worker buys a new car that gets a lot of attention, they are out there car shopping the next weekend. It is very emotionally destructive behavior. It can create financial difficulties, as well as having a tremendous impact on your ability to maintain healthy relationships.

Do you ever fall into this trap of comparing yourself to others? I do. It does not happen often, but will happen occasionally. I think understanding how useless the activity is and realizing the destructive force of this type of behavior can go a long way to helping you not fall into this trap.

One other thing I would suggest if you find yourself starting to make unhealthy comparisons is to make comparisons with yourself. I enjoy running and competing in triathlons. I have been doing it for years. The funny thing is that I am pathetically slow. I literally have finished races after the organizers have packed up and left, but I always finish.

If I were to compare myself to other athletes, I would have gotten discouraged and quit long ago. I don't ever compare myself to other athletes. Instead, I compare my performance to my own personal goals. If I run a little faster today than I did yesterday, I consider that a smashing success.

If I don't run a little faster, I may not necessarily view it as a failure. It just identifies that I may need to change how I am training.

I certainly don't have all of the answers in life, but I am pretty sure comparing yourself to others will not benefit you in any way. Yes, it may awaken your competitive spirit and you may push a little harder, but when will you ever be satisfied? What is the point of progressing if you are never going to take a moment to appreciate where you are?

I have regularly encouraged you to seek self-improvement in this book, and I assure you that will be a topic to come up in the future as well. I also want to make sure you appreciate where you are in life. The fact you are here reading about this particular topic leads me to believe you have made some pretty good decisions in life. You may not be perfect, but none of us are. Take a moment and appreciate all you have done and all you have learned.

24232084R00086

Made in the USA
Lexington, KY
10 July 2013